Interactive Curves and Surfaces

A Multimedia Tutorial on CAGD

The Morgan Kaufmann Series in Computer Graphics and Geometric Modeling
Series Editor, Brian A. Barsky

Interactive Curves and Surfaces: A Multimedia Tutorial on CAGD
Alyn Rockwood and Peter Chambers

Jim Blinn's Corner: A Trip Down the Graphics Pipeline
Jim Blinn

Wavelets for Computer Graphics: Theory and Applications
Eric J. Stollnitz, Tony D. DeRose, and David H. Salesin

Principles of Digital Image Synthesis
Andrew S. Glassner

Radiosity & Global Illumination
François X. Sillion and Claude Puech

Knotty: A B-Spline Visualization Program
Jonathan Yen

User Interface Management Systems: Models and Algorithms
Dan R. Olsen, Jr.

Making Them Move: Mechanics, Control, and Animation of Articulated Figures
Edited by Norman I. Badler, Brian A. Barsky, and David Zeltzer

Geometric and Solid Modeling: An Introduction
Christoph M. Hoffmann

An Introduction to Splines for Use in Computer Graphics and Geometric Modeling
Richard H. Bartels, John C. Beatty, and Brian A. Barsky

Interactive Curves and Surfaces

A Multimedia Tutorial on CAGD

Alyn Rockwood
Arizona State University

Peter Chambers
VLSI Technology, Inc.

Morgan Kaufmann Publishers, Inc.
San Francisco, California

Sponsoring Editor	Michael B. Morgan
Production Manager	Yonie Overton
Production Editor	Elisabeth Beller
Text Design	Rebecca Evans & Associates
Cover Design	Ross Carron Design
Copyeditor	Ken DellaPenta
Proofreader	Jennifer McClain
Composition	Nancy Logan
Illustration	Cherie Plumlee
Indexer	Ted Laux
Printer	Courier Corporation

Morgan Kaufmann Publishers, Inc.
Editorial and Sales Office
340 Pine Street, Sixth Floor
San Francisco, CA 94104-3205
USA

Telephone	415/392-2665
Facsimile	415/982-2665
E-mail	mkp@mkp.com
WWW	http://www.mkp.com

Order toll free   800/745-7323

Library of Congress Cataloging-in-Publication Data is available for this book.

ISBN 1-55860-405-7

Alyn Rockwood

For Mary, who was the first to know this book should exist

For the many students whose need stimulated this book

Peter Chambers

For my parents, for their endless encouragement and support

Contents

Topic 3: The Bézier Curve   31

The behavior and characteristics of this fundamental curve.

Topic 4: Interpolation   59

*Interpolating curves are designed to run through a set of
existing points. Common types are introduced.*

Topic 5: Blossoms   75

*Blossoms provide an intuitive method for creating Bézier
and B-spline curves.*

Topic 6: The B-Spline Curve   93

The B-spline curve is a very popular curve in industry today and is covered in detail.

Topic 7: Rational Curves   119

Rational curves introduce the idea of associating weights with the control points. This permits greater variety in the curve forms.

Topic 8: Surfaces   **133**

*This topic extends CAGD from two to three dimensions,
creating curved surfaces.*

Topic 9: Images and Applications   **143**

A gallery of applications and instructive images.

Preface

Welcome to *Interactive Curves and Surfaces*, where computer-aided geometric design (CAGD) comes to life with interactive, user-paced tuition.

This project began in the summer of 1994 as a way to improve the teaching of CAGD at Arizona State University. Seeing that some ideas are communicated much more effectively in an interactive, visual manner, Alyn Rockwood conceived the idea of an electronic book that would combine the best of the traditional CAGD texts with the power of graphical computers. In collaboration with Peter Chambers, the first tutorial was created and tried out by ASU students in early 1995. There was overwhelming enthusiasm, particularly with the interactive tools that illustrate the concepts of CAGD in a powerful, engaging way. The typical response was "Why wasn't this available sooner?"

We used the early version at the SIGGRAPH conference in 1995 and again found a great acceptance of the teaching method. The dry equations and static figures of conventional texts were brought to life, allowing exploration, experimentation, and a deep understanding for how CAGD really works.

This book and, importantly, the interactive tutorial, were written to demonstrate the graphical nature of CAGD in an entirely new way. The tutorial presents the material with a mixture of text, graphics, and interactive applications in which you can test the behavior of the curves. Hypertext, pop-up windows, and other navigation features help maximize your progress.

The tutorial presents the basic topics of CAGD, similar to those found in the traditional texts on the subject, including Bézier curves, B-spline curves, interpolating curves, and a variety of surface forms. The properties, behavior, and use of these curves and surfaces are discussed in depth. A Topic on Preliminary Mathematics will assist readers with suitable background material, while the Topic on Images and Applications illustrates uses of CAGD in science and industry. Newer, more advanced material, such as Gregory patches, implicit curves and surfaces, and non-rectangular patches, is also included.

The intent is to provide a primer on CAGD for final-year undergraduate or first-year postgraduate study. This one text will provide the bulk of the required material for a one-semester course on CAGD. The tutorial is also perfectly suited for individual study by people wishing a knowledge of the principles of CAGD. Readers are expected to have some background in algebra, geometry, and calculus. We have found that the interactive nature of the tutorial provides rapid familiarity of material that is both graphical and dynamic, with greatly enhanced comprehension as a result.

Students, architects, engineers, programmers, designers, and many others will gain a strong insight into the background of the curves and surfaces in popular use today.

With this electronic book, you will

■ become familiar with standard ways of creating curves and surfaces, including Bézier curves, B-splines, and parametric surface patches,

■ understand the mathematical tools behind the generation of these objects and the development of computer-based CAGD algorithms,

■ explore the behavior and characteristics of the most popular CAGD curves with interactive test benches,

■ understand the uses of computer-aided geometric design in science and industry.

We hope you enjoy this book and the new ground we're breaking together.

Acknowledgments

Both authors thank

- Mike Morgan, Marilyn Uffner Alan, and Elisabeth Beller at Morgan Kaufmann, for their patience as deadlines approached and for making this project possible.

- The reviewers, Spencer Thomas, Jim Miller, and Aristides Requicha, for their excellent comments and ideas. Without their hard work, this book would be far less than it is today. Thanks also to Jules Bloomenthal for his review of the early proposal.

- Shara-Dawn, for her diligent proofreading and the significant improvements in layout and flow she suggested.

- Professor Don Evans, director of the Center of Innovation in Engineering Education, of the College of Engineering and Applied Science, Arizona State University, for his help and encouragement.

The authors also appreciate the sponsorship of the U.S./Hungarian Science and Technology Joint Fund, in cooperation with Arizona State University, project 396.

Alyn and Peter

Installing
the Software

Interactive Curves and Surfaces is easy to install on your computer.

What You'll Need

■ A PC running Windows 3.1 or Windows 95. An Apple Macintosh with Windows emulation will also work.

■ A 486 or better processor, with at least four megabytes of memory. Eight megabytes is recommended for better performance.

Installing the Software: Windows 3.1

1. Insert disk number 1 in drive a: or b:.

2. From the Program Manager, select File...Run.

3. Type a:setup or b:setup, and click OK.

4. Follow the on-screen instructions.

Installing the Software: Windows 95

1. Insert disk number 1 in drive a: or b:.
2. Open the Control Panel by selecting Start...Settings...Control Panel.
3. Double-click Add/Remove Programs.
4. Select the Install/Uninstall tab, and click Install.
5. Follow the "Install Program from Floppy Disk or CDROM" instructions.
6. Follow the on-screen instructions.

To Run the Tutorial

Double-click the icon in the Interactive Curves and Surfaces group.

How to Use the Electronic Book

You are probably familiar with on-line help from other Windows applications. The Interactive Curves and Surfaces tutorial behaves the same:

- Use the left mouse button to click on highlighted words. Highlighted words may either display a popup window or take you to another section of the book. The left mouse button does almost everything. The mouse pointer turns into a hand 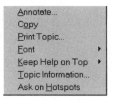 when it's over something you can usefully click on.

- If you're running Windows 95, use the right mouse button to bring up a menu of useful tasks:

Annotate...
Copy
Print Topic...
Font ▸
Keep Help on Top ▸
Topic Information...
Ask on Hotspots

From this menu, you may copy text to the clipboard, search for a topic, print a topic, or do some other tasks.

- The buttons along the top edge of the screen are standard on-line help controls, but notice the exit button ▭ Exit ▭, which exits the book, and the browse buttons ▭ << ▭ >> ▭. These provide a linear study flow through the book, presenting material in a logical sequence of steps.

- The interactive applications are started by clicking their graphical symbol. Once running, the applications are controlled separately from the book. Each has its own controls and instructions.

Introduction to CAGD

IN THIS TOPIC, YOU WILL LEARN

- what CAGD is about,
- some of the history of CAGD,
- about some typical applications of CAGD tools.

What CAGD Is All About

Computer-aided geometric design (CAGD) is a new field that initially developed to bring the advantages of computers to industries such as

- automotive
- aerospace
- shipbuilding

CAGD expanded rapidly and now pervades many areas, from pharmaceutical design to animation. We are surrounded by products that were first visualized on a computer. These products were modified and refined entirely within the computer; when the product entered production, the tools and dies were produced directly from the geometry stored in the computer. This process is known as *virtual prototyping*.

© 1993 Autodesk, Inc. Reprinted with permission.

Computer visualizations of new products reduce the design cycle by easing the process of design modification and tool production.

CAGD is based on the creation of curves and surfaces and is accurately described as curve and surface modeling. Using CAGD tools with elaborate user interfaces, designers create and refine their ideas to produce complex results. They combine large numbers of curve and surface segments to realize their ideas. However, the individual segments they use are relatively simple, and it is at this level that the study of CAGD is concentrated.

A Design Challenge: The Need for CAGD

When creating products and artwork, designers face tasks such as this: You are given two points in a plane and two directions associated with the points. Find the curve that passes through the points that is tangent to the given directions.

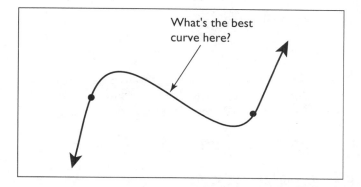

This is a simple pencil-and-paper task for anyone who is familiar with parametric forms, the types of curves used in CAGD.

CAGD tools are meant to be

- intuitive
- simple to use

Sometimes the mathematics underlying the tools becomes quite sophisticated, yet the result is meant to be easily understood and geometrically intuitive.

The technical person often benefits from these intuitive and visually related tools when considering deeper mathematical problems. The geometry of CAGD is very amenable to visual demonstration.

CAGD: From Points to Teapots

There is a natural progression of the geometry behind CAGD. With small incremental steps, it is possible to describe complex objects in terms of simple primitives, such as points and lines.

Control Points: The Start of CAGD

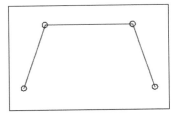

Take four points in a plane and connect them to form a polygon. The points are known as *control points*,[1] and the polygon as the *control polygon*.[2] The control points and polygon determine the approximate shape of the curve to be formed.

A CAGD Favorite: The Bézier Curve

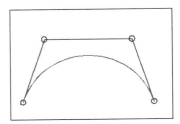

A special curve known as the *Bézier curve*[3] may be generated by the control points. Note that while the curve passes through the endpoints, it only comes close to the other points.

[1] Control points are points in two or more dimensions that define the behavior of the resulting curve.

[2] The control polygon is formed by connecting the control points in the correct order. The control polygon provides a crude analogy of the refined curve. Note that the control polygon is typically open (the ends are not coincident), and it may self-intersect arbitrarily.

[3] The Bézier curve, named after the French researcher Pierre Bézier, is a simple and useful CAGD curve. It is a very well behaved curve with useful properties, as you will discover in Topic 3, "The Bézier Curve."

Three-Dimensional Control Polygons for Surfaces (Control Meshes)

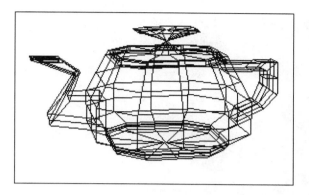

Bézier curves behave just as well in three dimensions as in two. This figure shows the control polygons for a three-dimensional object consisting of *Bézier patches.*[4]

Three-Dimensional Wireframe Model

When the Bézier curves are created and connected in three dimensions, a wireframe model of the object is produced.

[4]   A Bézier patch is a three-dimensional extension of a Bézier curve. It is formed by extruding a Bézier curve through space to form a surface.

Three-Dimensional Shaded Object

If the surface produced by the three-dimensional Bézier patches is illuminated and shaded, an object with a realistic appearance results. The Utah teapot, on display at the Boston Museum of Computer History, is a classic in CAGD and computer graphics.

The History of CAGD

Computer-aided geometric design has mathematical roots that stretch back to Euclid and Descartes. Its practical application began with automated machinery to compute, draft, and manufacture objects with free-form surfaces. Production pressures in the aircraft industry during World War II stimulated many new devices to enhance and accelerate design and manufacturing. For example, in 1944, Liming designed fuselage spars with a "superelliptic" method that could be implemented with an electromechanical calculator.

Shipbuilders also became interested in CAGD early on for many reasons. One example of their motivation may sound trivial but was a serious impediment to ship design. The only place large enough to draw full-scale plans for a ship was in the loft of the shipbuilders' dry dock. The huge drawings would warp and shrink in the moist air, causing very real manufacturing problems.

Computers provided the greatest stimulus because of their power to enable new ideas. In 1963, Ferguson developed one of the first surface patch systems by which individual curvilinear patches are joined smoothly to create the surface "quilt." He also introduced the notion of parametrically defined surfaces, which has become the standard because it provides freedom from an arbitrarily fixed coordinate system. Vertical tangent vectors can be defined by differentiation, for instance, which is not possible in explicit Cartesian form.

In the mid 1960s, automotive companies became involved in CAGD as a way to drive milling machines. Car bodies were designed by artists using clay models. Painstaking measurements produced data that could drive numerically controlled milling machines to produce stamp molds. The initial use of CAGD was to represent the data as a smooth surface for numerical control. It soon became apparent that the surfaces could be used for the design.

In 1971, Pierre Bézier reformulated Ferguson's ideas so that a draftsman without any extensive mathematical training could design a surface. Bezier's system, UNISURF, was used by Renault and became a milestone in the development of CAGD. It epitomized the difference between surface fitting and surface design. The purpose of design was to provide the draftsman, who had strong intuition about shape but limited mathematical training, with computer tools that empowered him or her to use the sophisticated mathematics of surface representation.

In the meantime, the mathematical underpinnings of CAGD continued to advance. De Casteljau examined triangular patches and developed evaluation techniques. Coons [Coons64] unified much of the previous work into a general scheme that became the basis of the early modeler PDGS made by Ford. At General Motors in 1974, Gordon and Riesenfeld exploited the properties of B-spline curves and surfaces for design.

Driven primarily by the automotive, shipbuilding, and aerospace industries, both the mathematics of CAGD and the designer interface tools continued to improve through the 1970s. The first CAGD conference was organized by Barnhill and Riesenfeld in 1974, where the term "CAGD" was first used [Barnhill74].

In the 1980s, the power and versatility of computer-aided designing seemed suddenly to be discovered by anyone who had a free-form geometric surface application. Industrial designers were smitten with the power of computer design, and many commercial modelers became the basis of several substantial applications, including CATIA, EUCLID, STRIM, ANVIL, and GEOMOD. Geoscience used CAGD methods to represent seismic horizons; computer graphics designers modeled their objects with surfaces, as did molecule designers for pharmaceuticals. Architects discovered CAGD, word processing and drafting programs based their interface protocols on free-form curves (*PostScript*[5]), and even moviemakers discovered the power of animating with such surfaces, beginning with *TRON*, continuing through *Jurassic Park*,[6] and beyond.

[5] PostScript is a proprietary page description language used by typesetters to define elements of printed text, including letter outlines, text layout, and graphical images.

[6] *Jurassic Park* made extensive use of CAGD and computer graphics to visualize animated objects.

What Has Been Accomplished in This Topic

The ideas and principles behind CAGD have been introduced, together with the classic example of surface patch use, the Utah teapot. The short but significant history of CAGD has been summarized.

Preliminary Mathematics

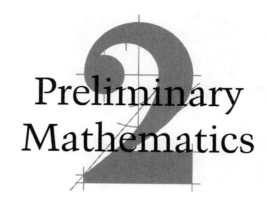

IN THIS TOPIC, YOU WILL LEARN

- the basic math needed for the rest of the book,

- an overview of parametric forms, a convenient way of describing curves and surfaces,

- the idea of continuity, to ensure that curves and surfaces join together smoothly,

- an illustration of linear interpolation, one of the most fundamental concepts in CAGD.

The Mathematics of CAGD

CAGD treats points, lines, and surfaces as mathematical objects, described geometrically in two- or three-dimensional space.

This book develops the mathematics in a step-by-step fashion and does not demand a rigorous mathematical background. It is recommended that the reader be familiar with the following topics:

■ geometry of points, lines, and planes

■ equations in parametric form

■ basic calculus

Parametric Forms

CAGD relies on parametric forms to describe curves and surfaces. Many students of CAGD do not initially appreciate the subtlety and importance of this form. If you are confident with parametric forms then you may skip to the section on continuity.

The Parametric Curve

Typically, when a student takes mathematics, a curve is presented as a graph of a function f(x).

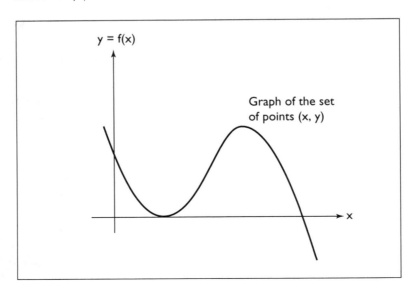

As x is varied, y = f(x) is computed by the function f, and the pair of coordinates (x, y) sweeps out the curve. This is called the *explicit* form of the curve.

From a design standpoint the explicit form is deficient in several ways.

Single-Valued

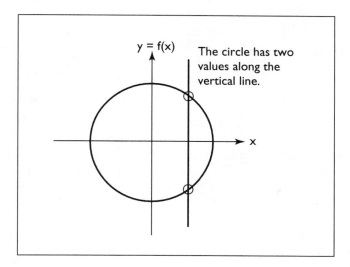

The curve is single-valued along any line parallel to the y axis. For example, only parts of the circle may be defined explicitly.

Infinite Slope

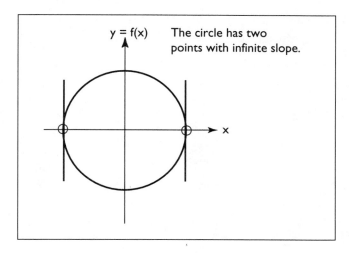

An explicit curve cannot have infinite slope; the derivative $f'(x)$ is not defined parallel to the y axis. Hence there are two points on the circle that cannot be defined.

Transformation Problems

Any transformation, such as rotation or shear, may cause an explicit curve to violate the two points above.

The parametric form of a curve is not subject to these limitations. Moreover, it provides a method, known as *parameterization*,[1] that defines motion on the curve. Motion on the curve refers to the way that the point (x, y) traces out the curve.

Defining the Parametric Curve

A parametric curve that lies in a plane is defined by two functions, $x(t)$ and $y(t)$, which use the independent parameter t. $x(t)$ and $y(t)$ are coordinate functions, since their values represent the coordinates of points on the curve. As t varies, the coordinates $(x(t), y(t))$ sweep out the curve. As an example consider the two functions:

$$x(t) = \sin(t), \ y(t) = \cos(t). \tag{2.1}$$

As t varies from zero to 2π, a circle is swept out by $(x(t), y(t))$.

[1] Parameterization uses an independent parameter or variable to compute points on the curve. It gives the "motion" of a point on the curve.

The Parametric Circle, t = 0.16 (approximately 57 degrees)

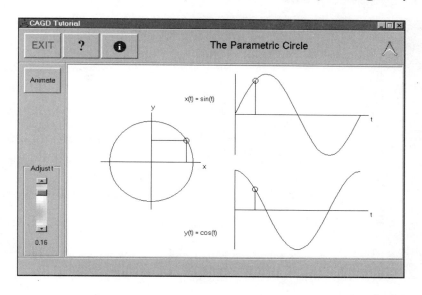

The Parametric Circle, t = 0.33 (approximately 118 degrees)

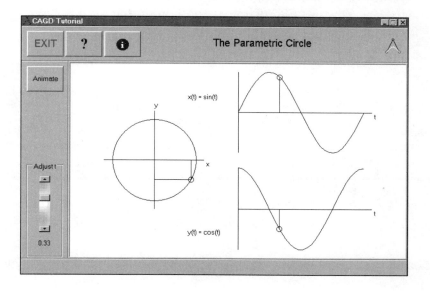

The Parametric Circle, t = 0.67 (approximately 241 degrees)

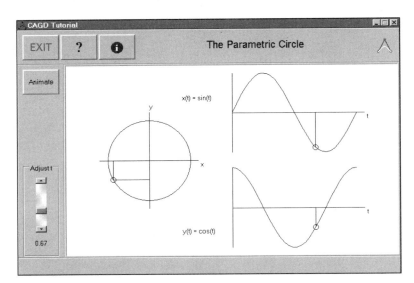

CAGD deals primarily with *polynomial*[2] or *rational functions*,[3] not trigonometric functions as shown in the examples above. For example, the circle can also be given by allowing t to vary from $-\infty$ to ∞ in the following functions:

$$x(t) = \frac{2t}{(1 + t^2)}, \ y(t) = \frac{(1 - t^2)}{(1 + t^2)}.$$ (2.2)

As an exercise, verify for yourself that the functions in equation 2.2 do indeed generate a circle. Plot points (x(t), y(t)) or write a program to do this for you.

Both equation 2.1 and equation 2.2 yield circles, so how do they differ? It is the parameterization. The motion of the point (x(t), y(t)) is different, even if the paths (the circles) are the same.

[2]   A polynomial is a function of the form
$p(t) = a_0 + a_1 t + a_2 t^2 + ... + a_n t^n$, where the a_i are scalars or vectors.

[3]   A rational function is made by dividing one polynomial by another, for example:
$$r(t) = \frac{1 - 2t + 3t^3 + t^4}{1 - 2t^2}.$$

A rational function may contain vector coefficients only within the numerator.

A good physical model for parametric curves is that of a *moving particle*.[4] The parameter t represents time. At any time t the position of the particle is (x(t), y(t)). Two paths (curves) may be identical even though the motion (parameterization) is different.

Parametric curves are not constrained to be single-valued along any line (recall the single-valued deficiency of the explicit form), and the slope of a parametric curve segment may be defined vertically. The slope is given by the *tangent line*[5] at any point, computed by finding the *derivative vector*[6] (x'(t), y'(t)) at any point t. This vector determines the speed at which the point traces out the curve as t changes.

Curves defined by points whose speed may drop to zero do cause problems that will be considered later under the discussion of continuity.

[4] As the parameter t changes, the coordinate point (x(t), y(t)) traces the curve. This point can be thought of as a particle that moves under the influence of changes in the value of the parameter t.

[5] The tangent line to a curve is the straight line that gives the curve's slope at a point. This is deduced from the derivative of the curve at the point.

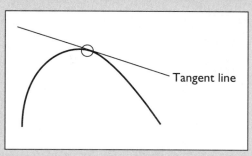

Tangent line

[6] The derivative vector (x'(t), y'(t)) at the point t is found by differentiating the functions x(t) and y(t) with respect to t.

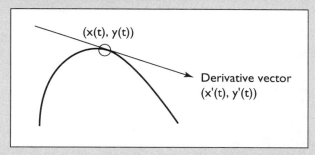

(x(t), y(t))

Derivative vector
(x'(t), y'(t))

Consider the parametric curve given by these two coordinate functions:

$$x(t) = 6t - 9t^2 + 4t^3,$$

$$y(t) = 4t^3 - 3t^2.$$

(2.3)

Bézier Tangent Demonstration

The illustration below demonstrates the following for this parametric curve, as t varies between 0 and 1:

- The parameter t moves the point $(x(t), y(t))$ along the path of the curve.

- The point's speed varies as t varies. The speed is higher at the ends of the curve.

- The derivative vector changes in length, reflecting the variation in the speed of the point.

- In the demonstration, the curve crosses itself, which can easily happen with parametric curves.

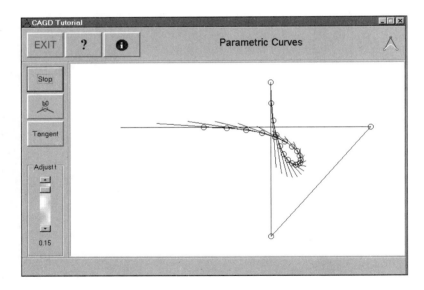

A convenient notation for equation 2.3 is

$$\mathbf{f}(t) = \begin{pmatrix} x(t) \\ y(t) \end{pmatrix} = \begin{pmatrix} 6 \\ 0 \end{pmatrix} t + \begin{pmatrix} -9 \\ -3 \end{pmatrix} t^2 + \begin{pmatrix} 4 \\ 4 \end{pmatrix} t^3.$$

(2.4)

Equations 2.3 and 2.4 are the same. We simply save on notation by writing the *basis functions*[7] only once, which are then multiplied by the appropriate vectors. When a vector is multiplied by a scalar, each coordinate in the vector is individually multiplied by the scalar.

In general, a parametric polynomial is written as

$$\mathbf{f}(t) = \mathbf{a}_0 + \mathbf{a}_1 t + \mathbf{a}_2 t^2 + \ldots + \mathbf{a}_n t^n, \tag{2.5}$$

where $\mathbf{f}(t)$ is a vector-valued function, and the $\mathbf{a}$'s are vectors. The vectors are not restricted to two dimensions. The $\mathbf{a}$'s might be vectors of three dimensions, for instance. In this case the function $\mathbf{f}(t)$ would have three coordinate functions $x(t)$, $y(t)$, and $z(t)$. The curve would be a curve in space, and the derivative $\mathbf{f}'(t)$ would be given by the vector of the derivative coordinate functions $(x'(t), y'(t), z'(t))$.

The general case described by equation 2.5 includes a constant term $(\mathbf{a}_0)$, which the example given by equations 2.3 and 2.4 does not have.

The Parametric Surface

As with curves, it is typical for the reader to have encountered surfaces explicitly as $z = f(x, y)$. Often called *elevation surfaces* or *terrain*, the height z is given at a point on the plane by computing $f(x, y)$. Such a surface definition shares the same flaws mentioned previously for curves:

- They must be single-valued for any point on the plane.
- They cannot have vertical tangent planes.
- Transformations may cause the above two difficulties.

The parametric form of the surface corrects these problems. In order to define a parametric surface, it is best to first define a parametric curve, and then sweep the curve through space to define the surface.

Consider a planar curve given by

$$\begin{aligned} x(t) &= 2 - 2t, \\ y(t) &= 2t - 2t^2. \end{aligned} \tag{2.6}$$

[7]   Here, the basis functions are 1, t, t^2, and t^3.

The coefficient for the basis function "1" is $\begin{pmatrix} 0 \\ 0 \end{pmatrix}$.

Or, in vector form,

$$\begin{pmatrix} x(t) \\ y(t) \end{pmatrix} = \begin{pmatrix} 2 \\ 0 \end{pmatrix} + \begin{pmatrix} -2 \\ 2 \end{pmatrix} t + \begin{pmatrix} 0 \\ -2 \end{pmatrix} t^2. \tag{2.7}$$

The curve given by $x(t)$ and $y(t)$ looks like this:

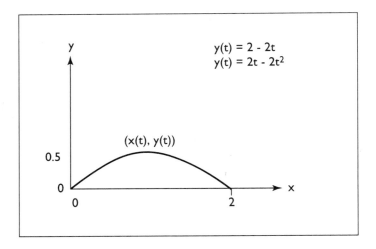

Here, the parameter t is limited to the range 0 to 1.

The curve becomes a surface in three dimensions if another parameter s and another coordinate function z are added. Consider, for instance:

$$\begin{aligned} x(s,t) &= 2 - 2t, \\ y(s,t) &= 2t - 2t^2, \\ z(s,t) &= s. \end{aligned} \tag{2.8}$$

When $s = 1$, the curve defined by equation 2.5 is produced on the plane $z = 1$. As this curve changes in s, it sweeps out a surface. A parametric surface may be thought of as a bundle of parametric curves; by fixing s or t on a surface, one single curve from this bundle is selected.

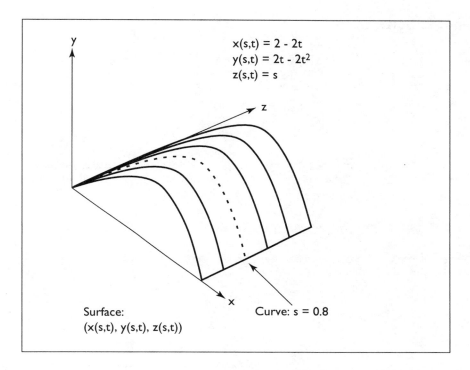

$x(s,t) = 2 - 2t$
$y(s,t) = 2t - 2t^2$
$z(s,t) = s$

Surface:
$(x(s,t), y(s,t), z(s,t))$ Curve: $s = 0.8$

In this figure, the planar curve is extruded through the z dimension to become a surface. When s = 0.8, the curve is produced as t varies between 0 and 1.

In equation 2.8, $x(s,t)$ and $y(s,t)$ have no terms in s, and $z(s,t)$ has no term in t. The terms are limited to simplify the example, but this is not typical. In general the surface may be written as the parametric polynomial

$$\mathbf{f}(s,t) = \begin{pmatrix} x(s,t) \\ y(s,t) \\ z(s,t) \end{pmatrix} \tag{2.9}$$

$$= \mathbf{a}_{00} + \mathbf{a}_{10}s + \mathbf{a}_{01}t + \mathbf{a}_{11}st + \mathbf{a}_{20}s^2 + \mathbf{a}_{02}t^2 + \mathbf{a}_{21}s^2t...$$

Bold letters indicate vector quantities. The indices of the **a**-vectors correspond to the parametric powers.

Parametric Derivatives

The derivative of a parametric curve, in the context of the way in which the curve is parameterized, was mentioned earlier. The derivative function of equation 2.3 is

$$\mathbf{f}'(t) = \begin{pmatrix} x'(t) \\ y'(t) \end{pmatrix} = \begin{pmatrix} 6 - 18t + 12t^2 \\ 12t^2 - 6t \end{pmatrix} = \begin{pmatrix} 6 \\ 0 \end{pmatrix} + \begin{pmatrix} -18 \\ -6 \end{pmatrix}t + \begin{pmatrix} 12 \\ 12 \end{pmatrix}t^2. \qquad (2.10)$$

The derivative function is itself a parametric curve of degree one less than the original curve. The derivative curve is called the *hodograph*.[8] The hodograph of $\mathbf{f}(t)$ reveals much about $\mathbf{f}(t)$, especially when viewed graphically.

The Hodograph of the Bézier Curve

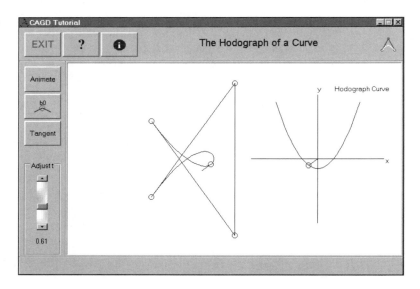

The hodograph curve on the right is derived from a series of tangent vectors, as shown in the next figure.

---

[8]   The word "hodograph" comes from the Greek *hodos* (road, path) and *-graph* (writing, writer). The curve was first devised by Sir W. R. Hamilton to plot the direction and velocity of moving particles.

The Vector Construction of the Hodograph

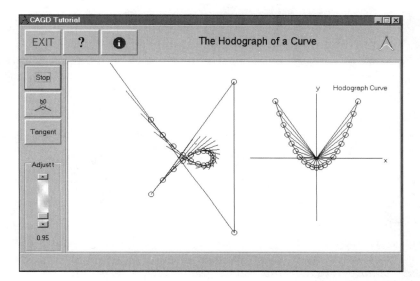

Notice in the hodograph demonstration that the derivative vector of $\mathbf{f}(t)$ is the vector from the origin to $\mathbf{f}'(t)$ in the hodograph. When the hodograph crosses the x axis, the original curve is parallel to the x axis; when the hodograph crosses the y axis, the curve is parallel to the y axis. The hodograph is discussed further in the section on continuity.

Recalling that a surface may be considered to be a bundle of curves in both the s and t parameters, it should not be surprising that the derivative of a surface must be given with respect to either the s or t parameter. For example, given a point, the derivative of the surface at that point with respect to the parameter s is simply the derivative of the curve embedded in the surface for a fixed t. At the same point on the surface there is another derivative with respect to t. So the derivatives at (s_0, t_0) are

$$\frac{\partial \mathbf{f}}{\partial s} (s_0, t_0) \text{ and } \frac{\partial \mathbf{f}}{\partial t} (s_0, t_0).$$

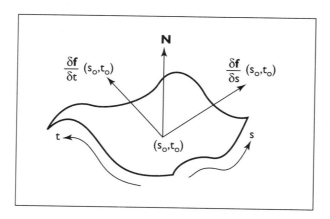

This figure shows the normal (**N**) to a surface, and the two derivatives with respect to the two parameters s and t.

The two derivative vectors define a tangent plane at the point (s, t). The *cross product*[9] of these two vectors yields the normal vector **N** to the tangent plane. **N** is also the normal to the surface at the point. This is very useful in applications that

[9] The Vector Cross Product: The cross product takes two input vectors and produces a third vector that is perpendicular to the input vectors.

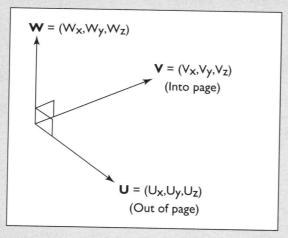

In the figure, the vector **W** is the cross product of vectors **U** and **V**, that is, **W = U × V**.

render the surface by computing light reflections using the surface normal. Typically the normal vector **N** is made to be unit length by dividing by its length, that is,

$$\mathbf{N} \text{ (normalized)} = \frac{\mathbf{N}}{\|\mathbf{N}\|}.$$

Continuity

The notion of *continuity*[10] was developed for explicit functions to describe when a curve does not break or tear. If it meets these conditions, it is described as C_0. C_0 continuity is defined by the popular description, "A curve is continuous if it can be drawn without lifting the pencil from the paper."

If the derivative curve is also continuous, then the curve is *first-order differentiable* and is said to be C_1 continuous. Extending this idea, it is said that a curve is C_k *differentiable* if the kth derivative curve is continuous.

Practically, this means that a C_1 continuous curve will not kink. Higher degrees of continuity imply a smoother curve.

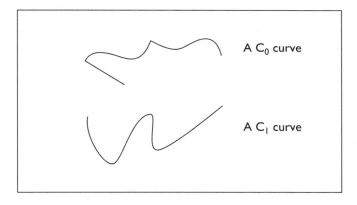

A C_0 curve

A C_1 curve

Two curves are shown here, one that is C_0 and one that is C_1. The C_0 curve has a kink, while the C_1 curve is generally smooth.

---

[10] Continuity implies a notion of smoothness, that is, curves that are not jagged and that do not break. Commercial applications of CAGD (for example, car body design) frequently require that curves and surfaces are continuous.

Unfortunately, continuity does not always result in the expected smoothness when viewed parametrically. The coordinate functions (such as x(t), y(t), and z(t)) may be first-order differentiable and still kink. All that continuity guarantees for parametric curves is that the motion of the particle (the parameterization) is smooth; there are no sudden jumps in velocity. It does not say that the path of the particle (the curve) is smooth.

The traditional notion of C_1 continuity does not, in fact, ensure much about the curve's properties. Imagine, for instance, a particle that travels in a straight line but has distinct jumps in velocity. It is not C_1, but the curve is certainly smooth. Conversely, it is possible to have a C_1 curve with a kink in it. This can occur when the velocity of the particle goes to zero, where it changes direction and starts up again. This is illustrated in the following figure:

A C_1 curve

Parameterization causes the particle's velocity to drop to zero here. As the particle starts moving again, it changes direction.

Mathematicians have developed the concept of a *manifold*[11] as a new way of describing continuity. In CAGD there is a simpler concept to achieve the same end. It is the idea of *geometric continuity*.[12] If a curve is C_0, it is G_0 continuous. If a curve's tangent direction changes continuously then it is G_1 continuous. Its magnitude may jump discontinuously, but the curve is still G_1. Hence a particle traveling at erratically changing speeds may still trace out a smooth curve if its direction changes smoothly. This is illustrated in the following figure:

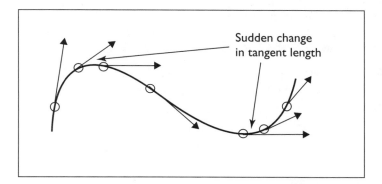

Sudden change in tangent length

[11] Informally, a manifold is a surface (or a hypersurface in n dimensions) that is a local deformation of Euclidean n-space at every point. Hence a 2-manifold looks like a curved plane locally.

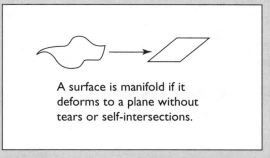

A surface is manifold if it deforms to a plane without tears or self-intersections.

If a surface is C_1 manifold, it implies smoothness, no tearing, no self-intersecting, and a few other more abstract notions.

[12] Geometric continuity introduces a notation that immediately tells the designer whether or not the curve is smooth.

If a C_1 curve has kinks because its derivative goes to zero at a point, then this curve will not be G_1, since the tangent direction changes discontinuously at the kink. Hence the notion of geometric continuity provides a useful way to understand the smoothness of a curve or surface.

EXERCISES

Describe physical situations in which

1. a particle travels with C_1 and G_1 continuity
2. a particle travels with C_1 but not G_1 continuity
3. a particle travels with G_1 but not C_1 continuity

Linear Interpolation

Given two points in space, a line can be defined that passes through them both in parametric form:

$$l(t) = (1 - t)\mathbf{b}_0 + t\mathbf{b}_1, \tag{2.11}$$

where

$$\mathbf{b}_0 = \begin{pmatrix} x_0 \\ y_0 \end{pmatrix} \text{ and } \mathbf{b}_1 = \begin{pmatrix} x_1 \\ y_1 \end{pmatrix}$$

the two points in space.

Thus $l(t)$ is a point somewhere in space, depending on the parameter t.

EXERCISES

4. What is the value of $l(0)$?
5. What is the value of $l(1)$?
6. What is the value of $l(\frac{1}{2})$?

Linear Interpolation between Two Points, t = 0.125

The screens captured for the interactive demonstration display only two places after the decimal point.

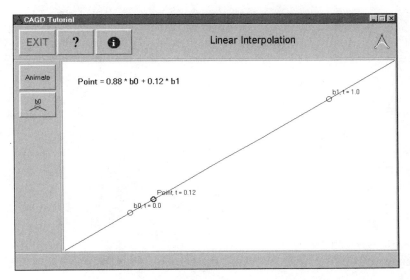

Linear Interpolation between Two Points, t = 0.25

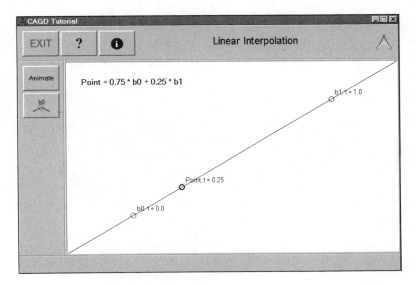

Linear Interpolation between Two Points, t = 0.5

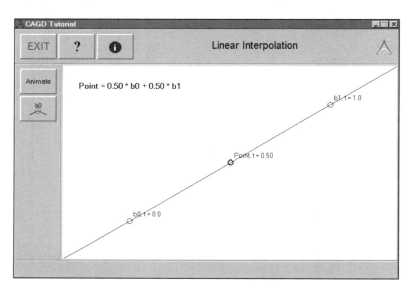

Linear interpolation is perhaps the most fundamental concept. All subsequent curves and surfaces are defined by repeated linear interpolation in some form.

Other forms of linear interpolation are possible. For example,

$$\mathbf{l}(t) = \frac{t\mathbf{b}_0}{10} + \left(1 - \frac{t}{10}\right)\mathbf{b}_1,$$

which also gives a straight line through the two points. Note that

$$\mathbf{l}(0) = \mathbf{b}_1 \text{ and } \mathbf{l}(10) = \mathbf{b}_0.$$

This is the same straight line (a linear combination of the two points), but it has a different parameterization. That is, the motion of a particle at t is different. In most cases it is preferable to start at t = 0 and end at t = 1.

Basis Functions

The final preliminary mathematics that is introduced is that of a polynomial basis. Polynomials such as equation 2.5 are written as a sum of coefficients and simple terms known as *monomials*.[13] If the monomials are considered as a collection P,

$$P = \{1, t, t^2, t^3, \dots, t^k\}, \tag{2.12}$$

then the question may be asked whether any polynomial of degree k can be written as a summation of terms, each a product of a coefficient and a basis function from P. If yes, then P is said to span the set of polynomials of degree k. Further, if P is the smallest set to span, then it is a basis for the polynomials of degree k. The set P is a *basis*,[14] called a *power basis*. If any monomial is eliminated from P, then not all polynomials of degree k can be written in terms of P.

There are other bases. Simple algebra allows us to rewrite parametric functions in another form. For example, consider this parametric polynomial of degree 2:

$$\mathbf{f}(t) + \mathbf{b}_0(1 - t)^2 + 2\mathbf{b}_1 t(1 - t) + \mathbf{b}_2 t_2. \tag{2.13}$$

This is written with combinations of the following terms:

$$\left\{ (1 - t)^2, \ 2t(1 - t), \ t^2 \right\}. \tag{2.14}$$

This can be rewritten in terms of the following monomials:

$$P = \{1, t, t^2\}, \tag{2.15}$$

as

$$\mathbf{f}(t) = \mathbf{b}_0 1 + (2\mathbf{b}_0 + 2\mathbf{b}_1)t + (\mathbf{b}_0 + \mathbf{b}_2)t_2. \tag{2.16}$$

Try this for yourself. In the example above, the coefficients **b** have a more geometrical and intuitive meaning. This meaning underpins the entire concept of designing with a computer.

---

[13] Monomials are single-termed polynomials. For example,

$$a_5 t^5, \ 6t^3, \ \begin{pmatrix} 5 \\ 3 \end{pmatrix} t, \ \begin{pmatrix} 2t \\ -2t^2 \end{pmatrix}.$$

[14] Given a space S of functions (a collection of functions such as polynomials, trigonometric, etc.), a set B is a basis if all functions of S are linear combinations of functions from B, and B is as small as possible.

What Has Been Accomplished in This Topic

The background to parameterized curves and surfaces has been covered in considerable detail. The hodograph visualized the behavior of the derivative of a curve and clarified the concept of the motion of a point on the curve.

Continuity was introduced to manage the boundaries between multiple curves or surfaces, and extended to include geometric continuity. Finally, linear interpolation was considered as a prerequisite for Bézier curves and blossoming.

The Bézier Curve

IN THIS TOPIC, YOU WILL LEARN

- what a Bézier curve is,
- the properties and behavior of the Bézier curve,
- how to create a Bézier curve,
- the de Casteljau algorithm for evaluation of a Bézier curve,
- subdivision, degree elevation, and differentiation of the Bézier curve.

Introduction to the Bézier Curve

The Bézier curve is a good place to start a study of CAGD. It underpins other concepts such as *B-splines*[1] and *surface patches.*[2] It is visually engaging and exhibits many desirable properties for design.

The Cubic Bézier Curve

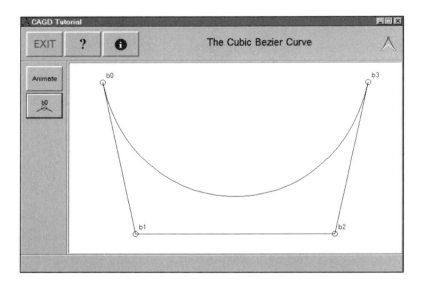

Mathematical Properties of the Bézier Curve

Consider the parabola that passes through (0,1) and (1,0) and is tangent to the x and y axes at these points:

---

[1] A B-spline is a highly controllable spline curve, a favorite of industrial designers. It is a piecewise polynomial, which may be described as a collection of Bézier curves.

[2] Surface patches are three-dimensional surface sections that may be combined to form solid objects.

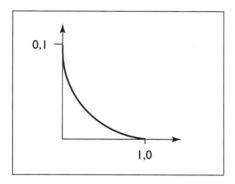

The parametric form of a parabola looks like

$$\mathbf{f}(t) = \mathbf{a}t^2 + \mathbf{b}t + \mathbf{c},\qquad(3.1)$$

where **a**, **b**, and **c** are vector coefficients. **f**(t) is a vector function with two components, that is, $\mathbf{f}(t) = (x(t), y(t))$. The above parabola can be written as

$$\mathbf{f}(t) = \begin{pmatrix} 1 \\ 1 \end{pmatrix} t^2 + \begin{pmatrix} -2 \\ 0 \end{pmatrix} t + \begin{pmatrix} 1 \\ 0 \end{pmatrix}.\qquad(3.2)$$

This can be rewritten as

$$\mathbf{f}(t) = \begin{pmatrix} 1 \\ 0 \end{pmatrix}(1-t)^2 + \begin{pmatrix} 0 \\ 0 \end{pmatrix}2t(1-t) + \begin{pmatrix} 0 \\ 1 \end{pmatrix}t^2.\qquad(3.3)$$

The reformation process is shown in the note below.[3]

---

[3] This parabola is defined parametrically by

$$y(t) = t^2$$

and

$$x(t) = 1 - 2t + t^2 = (1-t)^2.$$

In vector form, it may be expressed as

$$\mathbf{f}(t) = \begin{pmatrix} x(t) \\ y(t) \end{pmatrix} = \begin{pmatrix} 1 \\ 0 \end{pmatrix}(1-t)^2 + \begin{pmatrix} 0 \\ 0 \end{pmatrix}2t(1-t) + \begin{pmatrix} 0 \\ 1 \end{pmatrix}t^2.$$

This is exactly the same curve as equation 3.2, so what advantage is there in rewriting? The advantage lies in the geometrical meaning of the coefficients: (1,0), (0,0), and (0,1). These are called control points. Together, the control points form the control polygon.

Observe:

■ The curve passes through the endpoints of the control polygon.

■ The curve is cotangent to the control polygon at these endpoints.

The curve in this form is called the Bézier curve, and the observations hold in general for any coefficients. This means that if the coefficients are changed, the curve changes in an easy-to-understand way.

The Quadratic Bézier Curve

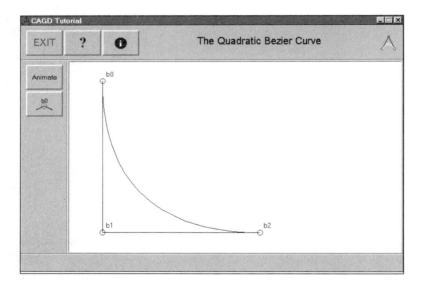

The general form for a quadratic Bézier curve is

$$\mathbf{f}(t) = \mathbf{b}_0(1 - t)^2 + \mathbf{b}_1 2t(1 - t) + \mathbf{b}_2 t^2. \tag{3.4}$$

This is a parabola exactly like equation 3.1, but it is rewritten so that the control points $\mathbf{b}_0$, $\mathbf{b}_1$, and $\mathbf{b}_2$ have geometrical significance as the control points of the parabola.

Bézier Curves of General Degree

The general form of a Bézier curve of degree n is

$$\mathbf{f}(t) = \sum_{i=0}^{n} \mathbf{b}_i B_i^n(t),$$

(3.5)

where $\mathbf{b}_i$ are vector coefficients, the now-familiar control points, and

$$B_i^n(t) = \binom{n}{i} t^i (1 - t)^{n-i}.$$

(3.6)

$\binom{n}{i}$ is the binomial coefficient; $B_i^n(t)$ are called the *Bernstein functions*.

Binomial Coefficients

The binomial coefficients, commonly derived from Pascal's triangle, may be computed:

$$\binom{n}{i} = \frac{n!}{i!(n - i)!},$$

(3.7)

for i, an integer ≥ 0.

Note that $\binom{n}{0} = 1$ and, in particular, $\binom{0}{0} = 1$.

Bernstein Functions

The Bernstein functions were originally devised by Bernstein to prove the famous Weierstrass theorem in 1912. They are formally given by

$$B_i^n(t) = \frac{n!}{i!(n - i)!} (1 - t)^{n-i} t^i.$$

(3.8)

They have many useful properties for curve generation.

The Cubic Bernstein Basis Functions

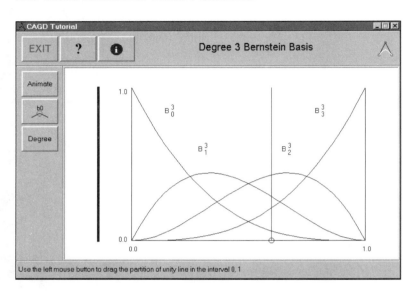

An important characteristic of the Bernstein functions is the partition of unity. This simply means that the sum of the functions is always one, for all values of t:

$$\sum_{i=0}^{n} B_i^n(t) = 1.$$

(3.9)

EXERCISE

1. Can you show that the Bernstein functions form a basis? That is, can you write any polynomial in Bernstein form? Pick a set of Bernstein polynomials, for example, with n = 3, then show

    $$\sum B_i^n = 1,$$

    for any value of t.

The collection of Bernstein functions for i = 0, 1, ..., n is the *Bernstein basis*.

The Bernstein basis is a key to understanding Bézier curves. Many of the important properties that make Bézier curves useful in design derive from these basis functions.

Characteristics of the Bézier Curve

Bézier curves have a number of characteristics that define their behavior.

Endpoint Interpolation

The Bézier curve interpolates the first and last points $\mathbf{b}_0$ and $\mathbf{b}_n$. In terms of the interpolation parameter t: $\mathbf{f}(0) = \mathbf{b}_0$ and $\mathbf{f}(1) = \mathbf{b}_n$. This property derives from the Bernstein functions, since at the endpoints the Bernstein functions are zero except at $\mathbf{b}_0$, $B_0^3 = 1$, and at $\mathbf{b}_3$, $B_3^3 = 1$.

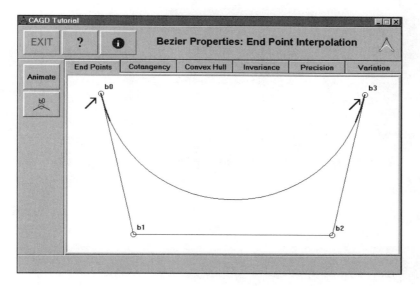

Tangent Conditions

The Bézier curve is tangent to the first and last segments of the control polygon, at the first and last control points. In fact,

$$\mathbf{f}'(0) = (\mathbf{b}_1 - \mathbf{b}_0)n$$

and

$$\mathbf{f}'(1) = (\mathbf{b}_n - \mathbf{b}_{n-1})n,$$

where n is a constant.

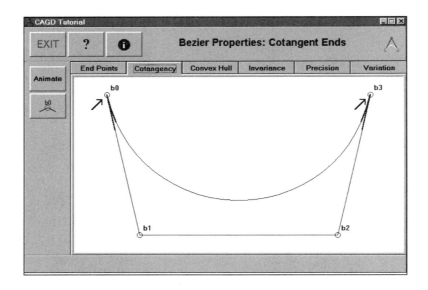

Convex Hull

The Bézier curve is contained in the *convex hull*[4] of its control points for $0 \le t \le 1$.

[4] The convex hull of a control polygon is the minimal convex enclosure of the control polygon.

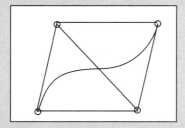

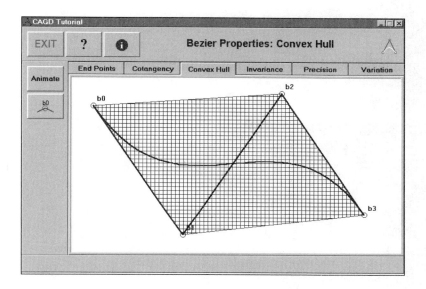

Affine Invariance

The Bézier curve is affinely invariant with respect to its control points. This means that any linear transformation (such as rotation or scaling) or translation of the control points defines a new curve that is just the transformation or translation of the original curve.

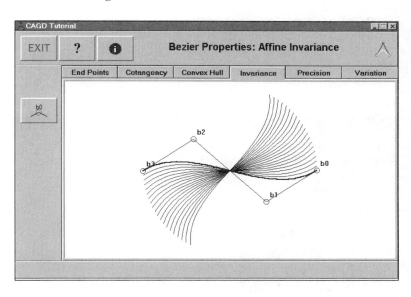

Variation Diminishing

The Bézier curve is variation diminishing. This means that it does not *wiggle*[5] any more than its control polygon; it may wiggle less. In this figure, notice that the straight line intersects the convex hull three times and also intersects the Bézier curve three times.

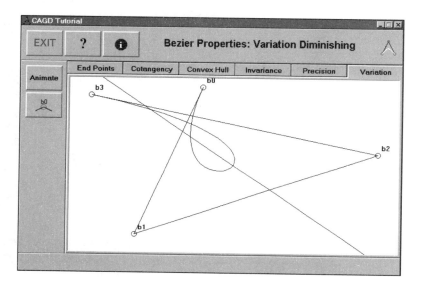

Linear Precision

The Bézier curve has linear precision: If all the control points form a straight line, the curve also forms a line. This follows from the convex hull property; as the convex hull becomes a line, so does the curve.

---

[5]   "Wiggle" means the way in which a curve or surface changes direction. This is more precisely expressed as a change in sign of the curvature of the curve or surface.

First step: Start with a simple cubic Bézier curve.

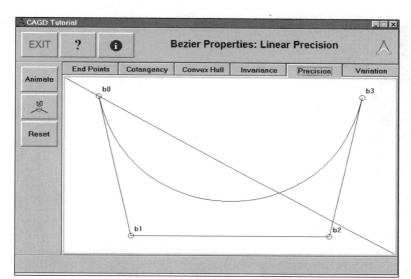

Second step: As the control points approach a line, the curve begins to flatten.

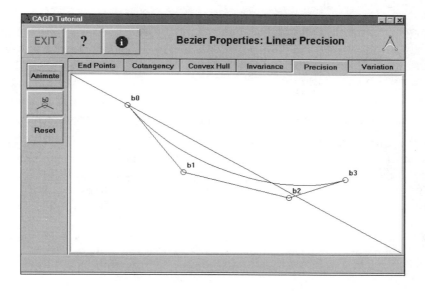

Last step: When the control points are colinear, the curve becomes a straight line.

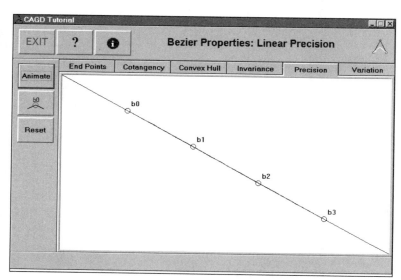

The de Casteljau Algorithm

Evaluation of the Bézier curve function at a given value t produces a point **f**(t). As t varies from 0 to 1, the point **f**(t) traces out the curve segment. One way to evaluate equation 3.5 is by direct substitution, that is, by applying the value of t to the formula and computing the result.

This is probably the worst method of evaluating a point on the curve! Numerical instability, caused by raising small values to high powers, generates errors.

There are several better methods available for evaluating the Bézier curve. One such method is the de Casteljau algorithm. This method not only provides a general, relatively fast, and robust algorithm, but it gives insight into the behavior of Bézier curves and leads to several important operations on the curves, such as the following:

■ *Computing derivatives.* The derivative of the curve gives the tangent vector at a point.

■ *Subdividing the curve.* It is sometimes necessary to take a single Bézier curve and produce two separate curve segments that together are identical to the original. To accomplish this, it is necessary to find two sets of control points for the two new curves.

The de Casteljau algorithm can be regarded as repeated linear interpolation.

As described in the section on linear interpolation in Topic 2, "Preliminary Mathematics," it is possible to interpolate between two points $\mathbf{b}_0$ and $\mathbf{b}_1$ with the equation

$$\mathbf{f}(t) = b_0(1 - t) + \mathbf{b}_1 t. \tag{3.10}$$

If $t = 0.5$, then $\mathbf{f}(t)$ is the midpoint of the line between the endpoints. Equation 3.10 is just a Bézier curve of degree $n = 1$.

De Casteljau's Algorithm for a Degree 2 Bézier Curve

This model may now be extended to handle a quadratic (degree 2) Bézier curve, as follows.

Step One

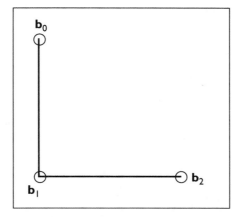

Consider the Bézier curve defined by three control points in the plane.

Step Two

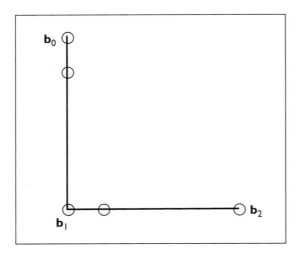

For a specific value of t, interpolate between adjacent pairs of endpoints. In this example, t = 0.2.

Step Three

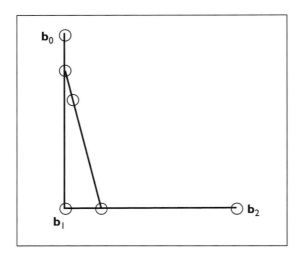

Using the same value of t (0.2), connect and interpolate between these two points. This point is on the degree 2 Bézier curve.

Step Four

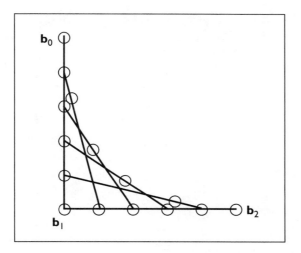

By repeating this procedure using a series of values of t, a set of points on the Bézier curve is produced. The point produced by the application of de Casteljau's algorithm traces out the Bézier curve.

String Art

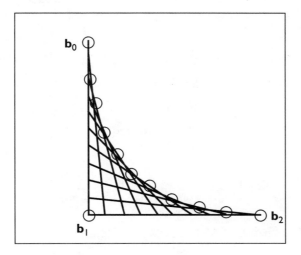

With finer granularity in the change in t, a picture similar to "string art," created by stretching string between nails on a board, is produced. Although the lines are straight, the boundary is a parabola, the Bézier curve. This process generalizes to Bézier curves of any degree; higher degree simply implies more levels of recursion.

A Demonstration of de Casteljau's Algorithm

Labeling the Bézier Curve for de Casteljau's Algorithm

To formalize de Casteljau's algorithm, a labeling scheme is needed that includes the points produced by the process of recursive linear interpolation. The scheme works as follows:

■ Each level of recursion is denoted by a superscript.

■ The control points are the zeroth level and do not need to be superscripted.

■ Each successive level of recursion has one less point than the previous level.

■ The final level $\mathbf{b}_0^n(t) = \mathbf{f}(t)$ is the point on the curve.

■ For any point, it may be shown

$$\mathbf{b}_i^j(t) = (1-t)\mathbf{b}_i^{j-1} + t\mathbf{b}_{i+1}^{j-1} \text{ for } i = 0\ldots n; \, j = 0\ldots i. \tag{3.11}$$

The Systolic Array: A Visualization of de Casteljau's Algorithm

One of the most important devices for dealing with curves is the *systolic array*. A systolic array is a triangular arrangement of vectors in which each row reflects the levels of recursion of the de Casteljau algorithm. The first row consists of the Bézier control points. Each successive row corresponds to the points produced by iterating with de Casteljau's algorithm.

Step One

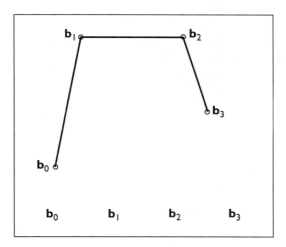

Step Two

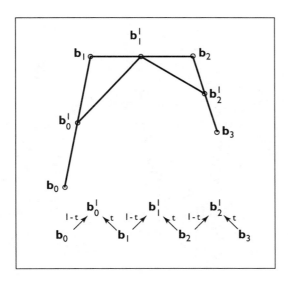

Step Three

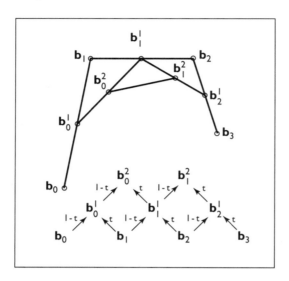

Step Four

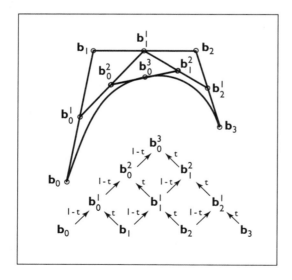

The point $\mathbf{b}_0^3$ is the point on the curve for some value of the parameter t.

Any point in the systolic array may be computed by linearly interpolating the two points in the preceding row with the parameter t; for example,

$$\mathbf{b}_1^2 = \mathbf{b}_1^1 (1 - t) + \mathbf{b}_2^1 t.$$

This process of linear interpolation is the fundamental operation in defining or evaluating a curve.

Subdivision of a Bézier Curve

One of the most important operations on a curve is that of subdividing it. The de Casteljau algorithm not only evaluates a point on the curve, it also subdivides a curve into two parts as a bonus. The control points of the two new curves appear along the sides of the systolic array. The new curves match the original in position, although they differ in parameterization.

Before the Subdivision

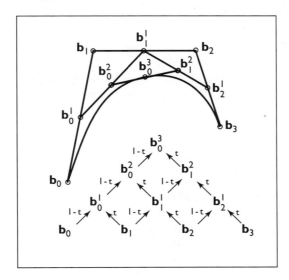

This is a cubic Bézier curve after three iterations of the de Casteljau algorithm, with the parameter $t = 0.5$.

After the Subdivision

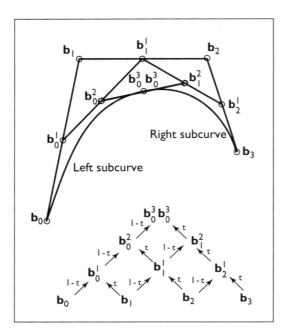

By using the left and right legs of the systolic array as control points, two separate Bézier curves are obtained that together replicate the original. The curve is subdivided at t = 0.5.

Uses of Subdivision

Design Refinement

Subdivision permits existing designs to be refined and modified. For example, additional curves may be incorporated into an object. This is accomplished by adding more control points for local control.

Clipping a Curve to a Boundary

One method of intersecting a Bézier curve with a line is to recursively subdivide the curve, testing for intersections of the curve's control polygons with the line. Curve segments not intersecting the line are discarded. This process is continued until a sufficiently fine intersection is attained.

The following figures from the tutorial illustrate the process of subdivision.

A Cubic Bézier Curve before Subdivision

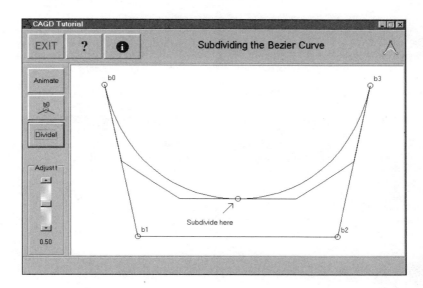

A Cubic Bézier Curve after Subdivision

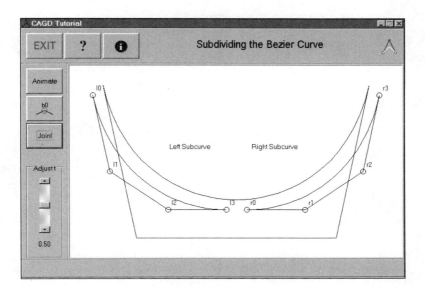

Higher Degree Bézier Curves

Bézier curves of any degree may be created. Degree 2 curves (quadratic curves) are the lowest degree useful. Many commercial applications and drawing packages use degree 3 Bézier curves (cubic curves) as a drawing primitive.

A Degree 8 Bézier Curve

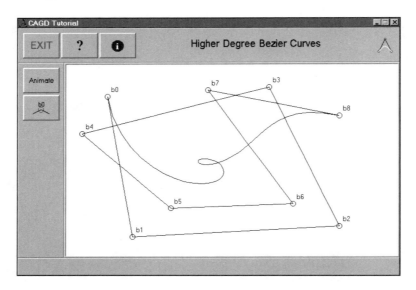

The Derivative of the Bézier Curve

It is a straightforward exercise in algebra to differentiate the Bézier function and then to formulate the derivative in Bézier form. The derivative of a Bézier curve of degree n is

$$\mathbf{f}'(t) = n\sum_{i=0}^{n-1} (\mathbf{b}_{i+1} - \mathbf{b}_i)B_i^{n-1}(t).$$
(3.12)

There is one less term in the derivative than in the original function. Also, the degree of the Bernstein polynomials is one less. The control points for the derivative curve are successive differences of the original curve's control points, having the form

$$\mathbf{b}_{i+1} - \mathbf{b}_i.$$

Consider the derivatives at the endpoints of the Bézier curve:

$$\mathbf{f}'(0) = n(\mathbf{b}_1 - \mathbf{b}_0), \text{ and } \mathbf{f}'(1) = n(\mathbf{b}_n - \mathbf{b}_{n-1}), \tag{3.13}$$

where n is a constant.

The tangent endpoint property is derived from these two derivatives. It may be seen that the derivatives (the tangents) at the endpoints are n times the first and last legs of the control polygon.

The hodograph of the Bézier curve is easy to construct in Bézier form. It is a Bézier curve with control points given by

$$\Delta\mathbf{b}_i = \mathbf{b}_{i+1} - \mathbf{b}_i, \, i = 0,1,\dots,n - 1. \tag{3.14}$$

The Hodograph of the Bézier Curve with Its Control Polygon

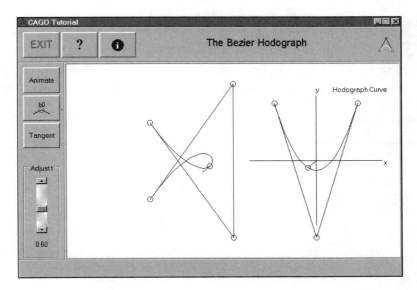

As before, the hodograph is created by plotting a series of tangent vectors of the original Bézier curve.

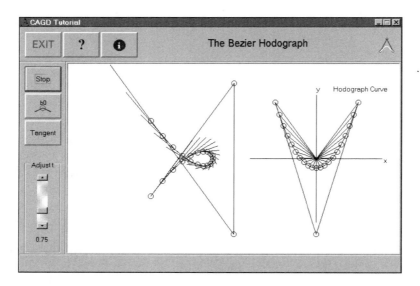

Continuity of the Bézier Curve

Earlier discussions on continuity focused on the differences between C_1 and G_1 continuity. The following figure shows a curve that is C_1 but not G_1; a particle tracing out the path of the curve would undergo a sudden reversal of direction at the kink, so the curve is not G_1. However, its hodograph is smooth, which makes the curve C_1.

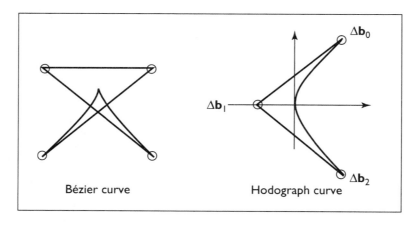

Bézier curve   Hodograph curve

Notice how the derivative goes to zero at the kink of the curve. This permits a smooth hodograph, without a smooth curve. Clearly, the superior measure of smoothness provided by geometric continuity is desirable.

Consider now the composite curve shown below. There are two Bézier curves attached at the point A. The composite curve is not C_1 at A since the derivative jumps in magnitude. The direction of the derivative does not change, however, and its path is smooth; it is G_1.

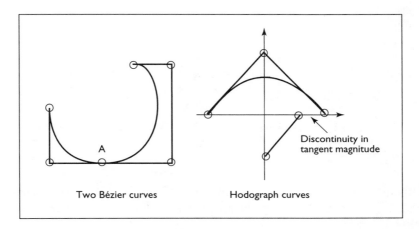

Two Bézier curves   Hodograph curves

The tangent vector (derivative) of the composite curve undergoes a discontinuous step in magnitude at the point where the two Bézier curves join.

Degree Elevation of the Bézier Curve

Any polynomial of degree n can be thought of as having higher degree terms than n if the coefficients are zero. For instance,

$$\mathbf{a}_0 + \mathbf{a}_1 t = \mathbf{a}_0 + \mathbf{a}_1 t + 0t^2 + 0t^3 + \ldots$$

This may seem pointless to do in standard polynomial form, but if the polynomial is in Bézier form, the coefficients of the higher degree polynomial are generally not zero. That means, for example, that the parabola

$$\mathbf{b}(t) = \begin{pmatrix} 0 \\ 1 \end{pmatrix} B_0^2(t) + \begin{pmatrix} 0 \\ 0 \end{pmatrix} B_1^2(t) + \begin{pmatrix} 1 \\ 0 \end{pmatrix} B_2^2(t) \tag{3.15}$$

has a cubic form:

$$\mathbf{b}(t) = \begin{pmatrix} 0 \\ 1 \end{pmatrix} B_0^3(t) + \begin{pmatrix} 0 \\ 0.33 \end{pmatrix} B_1^3(t) + \begin{pmatrix} 0.33 \\ 0 \end{pmatrix} B_2^3(t) + \begin{pmatrix} 1 \\ 0 \end{pmatrix} B_3^3(t). \tag{3.16}$$

This is identical in shape and in parameterization to the quadratic form.

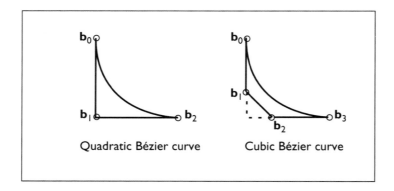

Quadratic Bézier curve   Cubic Bézier curve

This figure shows the quadratic and cubic forms for the same Bézier curve. The degree of the curve has been elevated without changing its shape or parameterization.

This means that if the cubic Bézier curve in the figure above is written as a standard polynomial, it would have one zero coefficient ($\mathbf{a}_3$), but in Bézier form, none of the control points ($\mathbf{b}_i$) are zero.

The algorithm to find the Bézier curve of the next higher degree is called *degree elevation*. It proceeds as follows.

Given a Bézier curve of degree n with control points $\mathbf{b}_0$, $\mathbf{b}_1$, ..., $\mathbf{b}_n$, it may be proved that the control points for the Bézier curve of degree n + 1 can be found as follows:

■ $\mathbf{b}'_0 = \mathbf{b}_0$ and $\mathbf{b}'_{n+1} = \mathbf{b}_n$. The endpoints are identical.

■ $\mathbf{b}'_i = \dfrac{i}{n+1}\mathbf{b}_{i-1} + \left(1 - \dfrac{i}{n+1}\right)\mathbf{b}_i, \quad i = 1, 2, ..., n.$ $\tag{3.17}$

A Cubic Bézier Curve Elevated to Degree 5

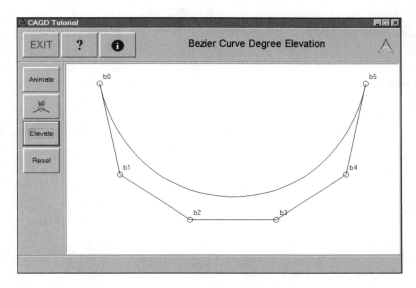

The following figure shows the same Bézier curve elevated to degree 19. The control polygon approximates the curve with greater accuracy.

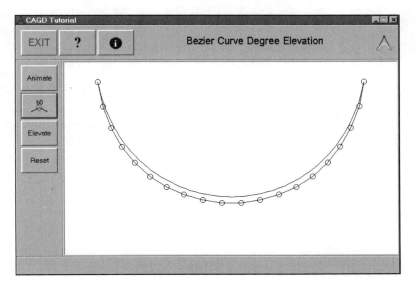

WHAT HAS BEEN ACCOMPLISHED IN THIS TOPIC

The Bézier curve has been covered in depth, with discussions of the properties of the curve. De Casteljau's algorithm generates the curve using iterated linear interpolation, providing a fast and stable way of creating Bézier curves. Subdivision, degree elevation, and differentiation of the Bézier curve completed the topic.

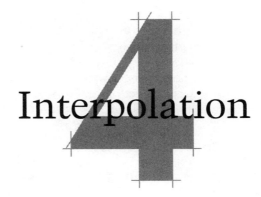

Interpolation

IN THIS TOPIC, YOU WILL LEARN

- ■ why interpolation is important,
- ■ how Lagrange interpolation works,
- ■ the use of Aitken's algorithm for computing interpolating curves,
- ■ the Hermite interpolant and its advantages.

Background to Interpolation

To *interpolate*[1] in mathematics means to estimate values between given known values. The Bézier curve, for instance, interpolates values between its endpoints. The other control points are not usually interpolated by the curve. There is, however, a polynomial form that interpolates all of the control points. It is the *Lagrange*[2] form. The Lagrange form is a good example of the more general topic of interpolation. It has connections to both iterated linear interpolation (for example, de Casteljau's algorithm) and nonuniform B-splines, which are introduced in Topic 6.

The following figure shows a cubic Lagrange curve interpolating four data points:

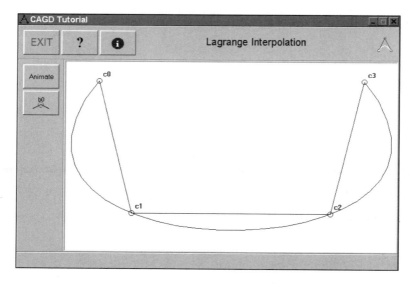

Based upon the discussion of the Bézier curve in Topic 3, the expected form of the Lagrange interpolation function is

$$\mathbf{f}(t) = \sum_{i=0}^{n} \mathbf{c}_i L_i^n(t), \qquad (4.1)$$

[1]   From the Latin *inter* (between) and *polare* (to polish): to enlarge (a book or manuscript) by insertion of words or subject matter.

[2]   Count Louis de Lagrange, 1736–1813, was a noted French astronomer and mathematician.

for some points **c** (to be interpolated) and some *basis functions*[3] L(t). From the study of Bézier curves and Bernstein basis functions, the Lagrange basis functions should rightly be expected to be the key to understanding the interpolation behavior.

In the Bézier case, interpolation of the endpoints occurred because at the parameter values corresponding to the endpoints (t varies from 0 to 1) all the basis functions are zero except the first and last, which are one. Thus **f**(0) and **f**(1) are exactly the control points. Applying this to the Lagrange case, basis functions are sought so that the ith basis function at some parameter t_i is one, and all others are zero.

In order to achieve this, a particular value of the parameter t must be associated with each point to interpolate **c**:

$$\mathbf{f}(t_i) = \mathbf{c}_i \text{ for all i.}$$

These values of the parameter t are called *knots* and may be selected as long as:

$$t_i < t_{i+1}.$$

Now consider the basis function that will give the interpolation property for all points:

$$L_i(t) = \frac{(t_0 - t)(t_1 - t)\dots(t_{i-1} - t)(t_{i+1} - t)\dots(t_n - t)}{(t_0 - t_i)\dots(t_{i-1} - t_i)(t_{i+1} - t_i)\dots(t_n - t_i)}. \qquad (4.2)$$

Notice that the numerator is the product of terms $(t_k - t)$, except where k = i. For any $t = t_k$ (k is not equal to i), the numerator is zero. Thus,

$$L_i(t_k) = 0.$$

This is part of what is sought. The other part follows by noting that if $t = t_i$, then terms in both numerator and denominator cancel and

$$L_i(t_i) = 1.$$

This is exactly what is needed; this means that

$$\mathbf{f}(t_i) = \mathbf{c}_i \text{ for all i.}$$

---

[3] Recall that given a space S of functions (a collection of functions such as polynomials, trigonometric, etc.), a set B is a basis if all functions of S are combinations of functions from B, and B is as small as possible.

This can be seen graphically in the following figure, which shows a cubic Lagrange basis with knots

$$t_0 = 0, t_1 = \frac{1}{3}, t_2 = \frac{2}{3}, \text{ and } t_3 = 1.$$

The following figure shows the cubic Lagrange basis functions:

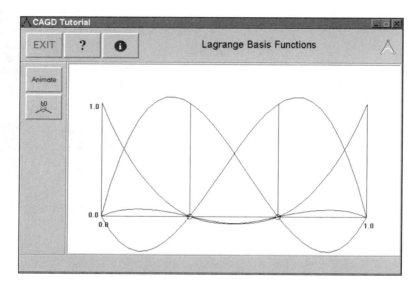

Notice how the basis functions are one at exactly one knot and zero at the others. This is the condition for interpolation.

Comparison of the Bernstein and Lagrange Basis Functions

Endpoint Interpolation

Where the Bézier curve interpolates the first and last points b_0 and b_n, the Lagrange basis causes interpolation of every control point **c**.

Tangent Conditions

The Bézier curve is tangent to the first and last segments of the control polygon, at the first and last control points. The Lagrange form does not have this property.

Affine Invariance

The Lagrange interpolant is affinely invariant with respect to its control points. This means that any linear transformation or translation of the control points defines a new curve that is just the transformation or translation of the original curve.

Convex Hull

The Bézier curve is contained in the *convex hull*[4] of its control points for $0 \leq t \leq 1$. Since the Lagrange basis does not possess the *partition of unity*[5] property, and because the basis functions may take negative values, the convex hull condition does not apply.

Variation Diminishing

The Lagrange interpolant curve is not *variation diminishing.*[6]

---

[4]   Recall that the convex hull of a control polygon is the minimal enclosure of the control polygon such that if two points are in the hull, then the line segment between is also in the hull.

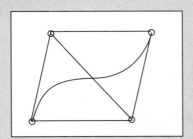

[5]   Recall for the Bernstein functions:

$$\sum_{i=0}^{n} B_i^n(t) = 1$$

and

$$B_i(t) \geq 0.$$

[6]   The Lagrange interpolant may well wiggle more than its control polygon. "Wiggle" means the way in which a curve or surface changes direction.

Linear Precision

Like the Bézier curve, the Lagrange interpolant has linear precision: If all the control points form a straight line, the curve also forms a line.

Despite the limitations of the Lagrange basis functions, they may be appropriate for some applications.

Before leaving the topic of Lagrange basis functions, there is something special to note: the basis functions depend on a knot sequence for definition. This was not true of the Bernstein polynomials; they are independent of any relation between control points and parameter space. In the following figures, selection of the knots can change the shape of the basis functions and the manner in which the interpolating curve responds. This will be seen again with B-spline curves.

The following figure shows a cubic Lagrange interpolating curve with a uniform knot sequence:

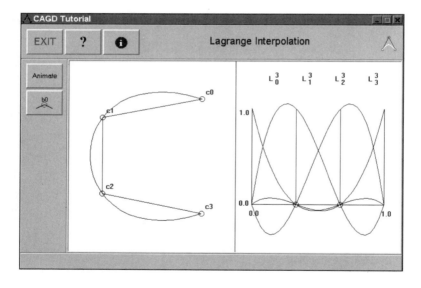

Now, the same set of data points is used but with a nonuniform knot sequence.

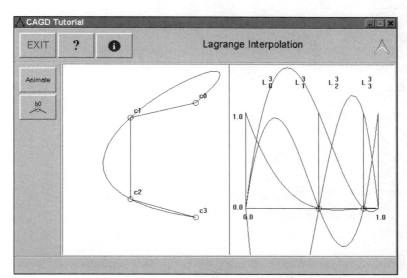

The shape of the curve can sometimes be quite difficult and unintuitive to control in the Lagrange form, especially compared to Bézier. Lagrange is not often used in shape design, but it provides a working method of interpolation.

EXERCISE

1. Can you give an example where interpolation is more important than design?

Evaluation of the Lagrange Curve

As in the case of Bézier curves, direct evaluation of a Lagrange interpolating curve is a poor approach; in fact, it's even worse than Bézier. Numerical instability is a major problem with direct evaluation of Lagrange; examine the basis functions $L(t)$ and look for places where division by zero may occur. Use of very small values is also a challenge.

Iterated linear interpolation again becomes useful. The analog of the de Casteljau algorithm in the case of Lagrange curves is the *Aitken algorithm.* Starting with a quadratic case, let the knot sequence be

$$t_0 = 0, t_1 = \frac{1}{4}, t_2 = 1.$$

The following figure shows the interpolation points and the knot sequence:

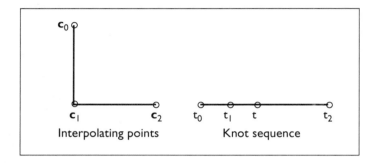

Find the point on the curve at $t = 0.5$. By linear interpolation from c_0 to c_1, a point is found on the extension of c_0-c_1, resulting in the following figure:

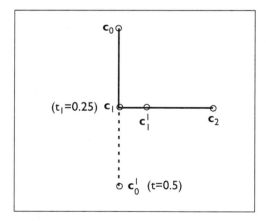

The point c_0^1 is interpolated from c_0 and c_1; c_1^1 from c_1 and c_2.

Finally, the point $\mathbf{c}_0^2$ is halfway along the line from $\mathbf{c}_0^1$ and $\mathbf{c}_1^1$:

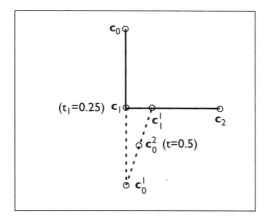

The pattern of iterated interpolation should be evident. Something changed from the first iteration to the second; examine the following examples.

The following figure shows an example of a quadratic Lagrange interpolating curve:

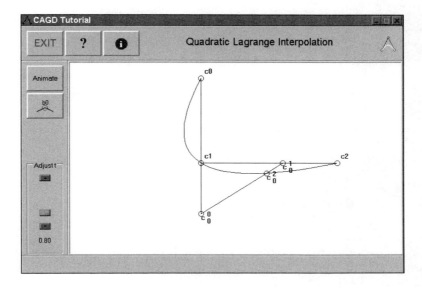

Now the same curve is shown with a different parameter value:

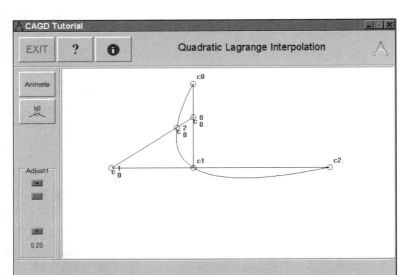

In these figures, a uniform knot sequence is used. It is easy to see that the first iteration computes

$$\mathbf{c}_i^1 = \frac{(t_{i+1} - t)}{(t_{i+1} - t_i)}\, \mathbf{c}_i + \frac{(t - t_i)}{(t_{i+1} - t_i)}\, \mathbf{c}_{i+1}, \; i = 0, 1. \tag{4.3}$$

It is less obvious that

$$\mathbf{c}_0^2 = \frac{(t_2 - t)}{(t_2 - t_0)}\, \mathbf{c}_0^1 + \frac{(t - t_0)}{(t_2 - t_0)}\, \mathbf{c}_1^1. \tag{4.4}$$

The second iteration uses a different knot-dependent weight than the first. In general, the Aitken algorithm is

$$\mathbf{c}_i^j = \frac{(t_{i+j} - t)}{(t_{i+j} - t_i)}\, \mathbf{c}_i^{j-1} + \frac{(t - t_i)}{(t_{i+j} - t_i)}\, \mathbf{c}_{i+1}^{j-1}, \; i = 0, \ldots, n - j; j = 1, \ldots, n. \tag{4.5}$$

The derivation of the points in Aitken's algorithm can be arranged in a systolic array. The difference between the de Casteljau array and Aitken's is that the weights change at each level in Aitken's. The weights are constant in de Casteljau's algorithm.

Here is an example with a nonuniform knot sequence:

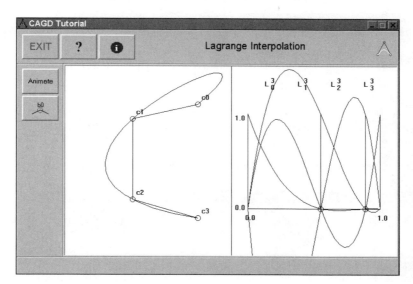

Hermite Interpolation

There is a very special interpolation form that is defined only for cubic curves. *Hermite*[7] curves interpolate to two points and two given tangent vectors. This can be useful for design and interpolation problems where slopes are given or can be estimated.

The Hermite curve is given by

$$\mathbf{h}(t) = \mathbf{p}_0 H_0(t) + \mathbf{m}_0 H_1(t) + \mathbf{m}_1 H_2(t) + \mathbf{p}_1 H_3(t),\qquad(4.6)$$

where $\mathbf{p}$ denotes the two endpoints and $\mathbf{m}$ the tangent vectors. The Hermite basis functions are given by

[7] Charles Hermite (1822–1901) was a famous mathematician.

$$H_0^3(t) = B_0^3(t) + B_1^3(t),$$

$$H_1^3(t) = \frac{1}{3} B_1^3(t),$$ (4.7)

$$H_2^3(t) = -\frac{1}{3} B_2^3(t), \text{ and}$$

$$H_3^3(t) = B_2^3(t) + B_3^3(t).$$

Here, the Hermite basis functions are given in terms of the *Bernstein basis functions.*[8]

The following figure shows the four cubic Hermite basis functions:

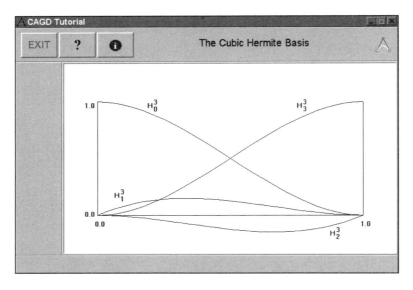

As with the other forms, at t = 0 all functions are zero, except the first:

$$H_0^3(0) = 1.$$

---

[8] $B_i^n(t) = \dfrac{n!}{i!(n-i)!} (1-t)^{n-i} t^i.$

This ensures the endpoint interpolation requirement. Similarly,

$$H_3^3(1) = 1,$$

which ensures that the curve interpolates the second endpoint. A unique feature of Hermite is that the derivatives are all zero at t = 0, except the first:

$$H_1^{3'}(0) = 1.$$

This means that at the first point $\mathbf{h}(0)$, the Hermite curve's derivative is defined entirely by the first tangent vector $\mathbf{m}_0$. Similarly, at $\mathbf{h}(1)$ the derivative is found from $\mathbf{m}_1$, since

$$H_2^{3'}(1) = 1.$$

When t = 1, the other three basis functions have zero derivatives. The following figures show the Hermite form and the equivalent Bézier form. Notice the similarities and the differences.

First, an example of the cubic Hermite curve, showing the Hermite form:

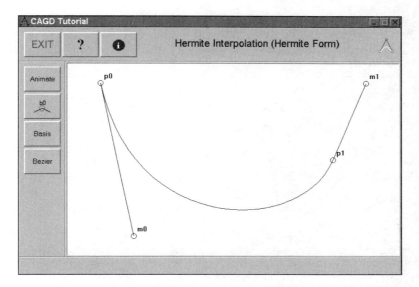

The next figure shows the same curve, but using the Bézier form:

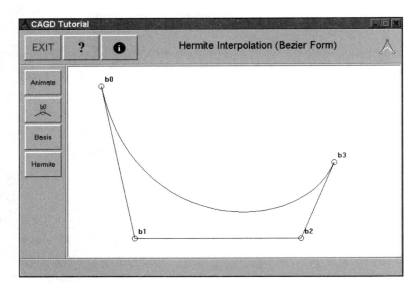

The Hermite form is convenient for interpolating data with slope information. The cubic pieces can be attached with shared endpoints and tangent vectors to create a smooth curve through a data set. This is illustrated in the following figure:

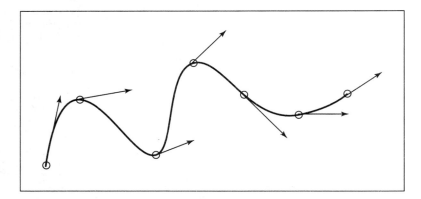

EXERCISES

2. What is the relation between the first tangent vector (at p_0) in a Hermite curve and the first leg of the corresponding Bézier curve's control polygon?

3. How would the **m** tangent vectors be selected if only a set of **p** endpoints is given? A smooth interpolant must be created.

4. Show that

$$H_0^3(t) = B_0^3(t) + B_1^3(t),$$

$$H_1^3(t) = \frac{1}{3} B_1^3(t),$$

$$H_2^3(t) = -\frac{1}{3} B_2^3(t), \text{ and}$$

$$H_3^3(t) = B_2^3(t) + B_3^3(t).$$

5. What properties does the Hermite form possess?

Other Interpolation Forms

There are other forms of interpolating curves. An important form that is beyond the scope of this tutorial is the interpolatory spline. It allows piecewise interpolation of data sets like Hermite, but with the constraint that the joins are C_{n-1} continuous, where n is the degree.

WHAT HAS BEEN ACCOMPLISHED IN THIS TOPIC

Two methods for producing interpolating curves have been discussed, providing a solution to a common problem: that of passing a smooth curve through a set of data points.

Blossoms

IN THIS TOPIC, YOU WILL LEARN

- what a blossom is, and the connection between blossoms and CAGD,
- the characteristics of blossoms,
- the application of blossoming to Bézier and B-spline curves,
- the uses of blossoms in CAGD.

Introduction

> *What's in a name? That which we call a rose, by any other name would smell as sweet.*
>
> —SHAKESPEARE, Romeo and Juliet

In some instances, the name given to an object has little importance. A fragrance, for example, does not depend on its name. This is not true in mathematics, however; labels are significant. Well-chosen notation serves not only as a tag, but also suggests how a concept is defined and used. This is especially true of a technique called blossoming. Its power lies in its ability to suggest fundamentals, algorithms, and theorems in CAGD through labeling. The theory of blossoms was introduced by Ramshaw and de Casteljau.

Blossom Basics

The basic principle of blossoming arises from *linear interpolation*.[1] Recall that $\mathbf{b}(0)$ and $\mathbf{b}(1)$ are points on the line segment at $t = 0$ and $t = 1$. Any point on the line is given by $\mathbf{b}(\mathbf{a})$. The distance from $\mathbf{b}(0)$ to $\mathbf{b}(\mathbf{a})$ is proportional to $|\,0 - \mathbf{a}\,|$. Similarly, the distance from $\mathbf{b}(\mathbf{a})$ to $\mathbf{b}(1)$ is proportional to $|\,1 - \mathbf{a}\,|$. It is very useful to think of $\mathbf{a}$ as a measure of how far a point travels from $\mathbf{b}(0)$ to $\mathbf{b}(\mathbf{a})$. For example, if $\mathbf{a} = 0.5$, then $\mathbf{b}(\mathbf{a})$ is halfway between $\mathbf{b}(\mathbf{a})$ and $\mathbf{b}(1)$.

The following figure recalls the introductory linear interpolation material in Topic 2, "Preliminary Mathematics." However, the figure here emphasizes the affine transformation between the linear space of $\mathbf{a}$ and the line segment $\mathbf{b}(0)$–$\mathbf{b}(1)$.

---

[1] Given two points in space, a line in parametric form can be defined that passes through them:

$$\mathbf{l}(t) = (1 - t)\mathbf{b}_0 + t\mathbf{b}_1,$$

where $\mathbf{b}_0 = \begin{pmatrix} x_0 \\ y_0 \end{pmatrix}$ and $\mathbf{b}_1 = \begin{pmatrix} x_1 \\ y_1 \end{pmatrix}$, the two points in space.

Thus $\mathbf{l}(t)$ is a point somewhere on the line between the two points, depending on the parameter t.

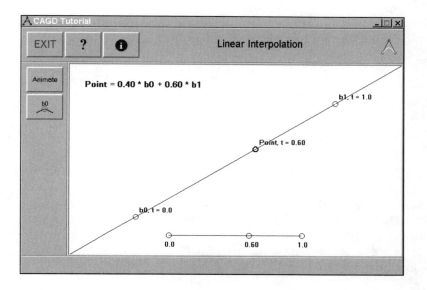

Notation

To further emphasize this relationship between **a** and **b**(0)–**b**(1), the functional notation is dropped and simply written **b**(0) = **0**, **b**(1) = **1**, and **b**(a) = **a**. **a** is spoken of loosely as the *affine distance*[2] from **0** to **a**.

Essentially, a point is designated by its parameter value **a** and the endpoints of the segment on which it lies, with the understanding that the point is obtained by linear interpolation along the line.

This is shown in the following figure, which clarifies the new nomenclature:

[2] The affine distance of a point **a** to a point **b** on a line **bc** is the ratio of the distances:

$$\frac{|\,\mathbf{ba}\,|}{|\,\mathbf{bc}\,|}.$$

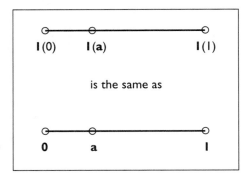

Next an important extension is made to the notation in order to describe two lines that share a point. This is done by adding an additional digit, as shown in the following figures. First, add the digits to the two individual lines. The first line is identified with a leading **0**; it goes from **00** to **01**. The second line has a leading **1**, going from **10** to **11**.

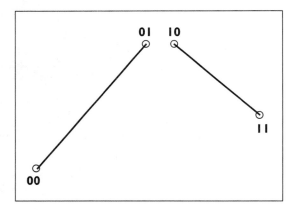

Next, bring the lines together so that they share an endpoint:

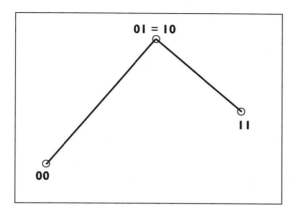

Note here (this is most important, even though it seems obvious) that point **01** and point **10** are identical.

When there was a single line, the point **a** was on the line from **0** to **1**. In the two-line figure, if the point **0a** is on the line from **00** to **01**, then where is the point **1a**? Clearly, on the new line:

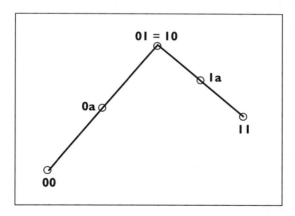

Point Ordering Is Not Significant

The next generalization comes from noticing that the order of the digits is not important: **0a** or **a0** can be used to identify uniquely the point on the first line. Therefore, the digits may be in any order:

01 ≡ 10,
a0 ≡ 0a,
a1 ≡ 1a.

Now consider a new line from **0a** to **1a**. Where is **aa**? It is the affine distance **a** between the line's endpoints, **0a** and **1a**. This is shown in the following figure:

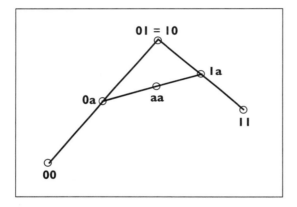

Furthermore it should be clear that **aa**, by its construction, is a point on a quadratic Bézier curve with control points **00**, **01**, and **11**. This follows from understanding de Casteljau's algorithm, which is based on repeated linear interpolation. The Bézier curve is shown in the following figure:

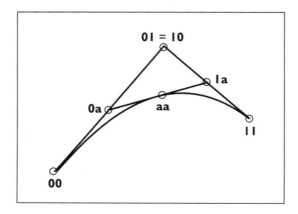

To add another control point, add another digit.

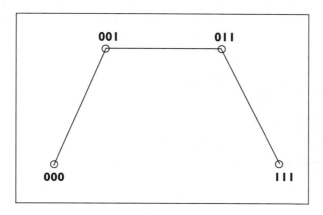

Where are the points **00a**, **0a1**, and **a11**?[3]

Here a convention is adopted of ordering the digits from smallest to largest. For example, **0a1** is preferred to **1a0**, so long as $0 \leq a \leq 1$. Sometimes commas are used to separate the digits, if required for clarity. The point **0,.5,1** is not **0.5 1**.

[3] The answer is best shown graphically:

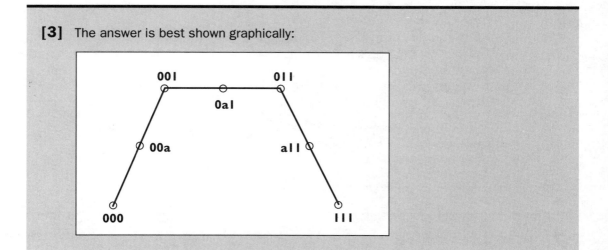

In the last figure, where is the point **aaa**? It can be found by recursive replacement. This is the so-called *blossoming principle*.[4] First, find **00a**, **0a1**, and **a11** on the appropriate lines. Then, find **0aa** and **aa1**. Finally, **aaa** may be found on the line between **0aa** and **aa1**:

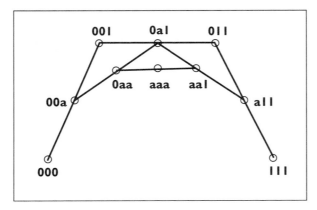

By construction, the point **aaa** is on the Bézier curve with control points **000**, **001**, **011**, and **111**:

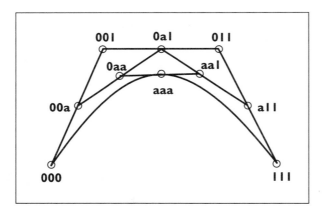

---

[4] Informally, the digit that differs between two blossoms is replaced with another value, giving the affine distance along the line segment for the new value.

Thus, **axx** is found on the line segment between **bxx** and **cxx**, an affine distance given by

$$\frac{|\,bxx - axx\,|}{|\,cxx - bxx\,|}.$$

EXERCISE

1. Draw five points and find the point **aaaa** for a degree 4 Bézier curve.

Summary of Blossoming from Linear Interpolation

The generalization of this method for a Bézier curve of any degree should now be clear. The principles generated thus far may be summarized:

1. There is a Bézier curve of degree n that is given by points of the form **aa....a**. There are n **a**'s.

2. The points are equivalent regardless of the ordering of the digits:
    a10 ≡ 01a ≡ 0a1.

3. The point **0...0a1...1** is an affine distance **a** along the line from **0...001...1** to **0...011...1**. In other words:

    $$\mathbf{0a1} = (1 - \mathbf{a})\,\mathbf{001} + (\mathbf{a})\,\mathbf{011}.$$

This is simple linear interpolation.

The History of Blossoms

It was proved by Ramshaw and de Casteljau that for every polynomial $P(u)$ of degree n, there is a unique function of n variables $p(u_1, u_2, ..., u_n)$ that has the three properties listed in the summary above. Ramshaw called this function the blossom of the polynomial $P(u)$. Quite often this blossom is given only as a list of its variables, as shown. The blossom notation suggests methods and algorithms naturally. The de Casteljau algorithm arose by recursively applying the principles until **a...a** was found.

The Formal Definition of Blossoms

To define a blossom, start with $P(u)$, a polynomial of degree d. For an integer $N \geq d$, the Nth blossom of the polynomial P is

$$\text{Blm}_N(P(u)) = p(u_1, u_2, ..., u_N), \text{ such that}$$

1. $P(u) = p(u, u, ..., u)$ (5.1)

     This property is known as *diagonal agreement*.

2. $p(u_1, u_2, ..., u_N) = p(\text{permute } u_1, u_2, ..., u_N)$ (5.2)

     This property is one of *symmetry*. The u values may be interchanged without modifying the blossom.

3. $p(..., as + bt, ...) = a\, p(..., s, ...) + b\, p(..., t, ...)$ if $a + b = 1$ (5.3)

This is the *multiaffinity* property.

Examples of Blossoms

1. $\text{Blm}_2(u^2) = u_1 u_2$.

2. $\text{Blm}_3(u^3) = u_1 u_2 u_3$.

3. $\text{Blm}_3(u^2) = \dfrac{(u_1 u_2 + u_2 u_3 + u_1 u_3)}{3}$.

4. $\text{Blm}_3(2 + 3u - u^2 + u^3) = 2 + (u_1 + u_2 + u_3)$

$$+ \frac{(u_1 u_2 + u_2 u_3 + u_1 u_3)}{3} + u_1 u_2 u_3.$$

For any polynomial P and integer N, there exists one and only one blossom. Generally speaking, however, the blossom properties are more important than the blossom itself.

EXERCISES

2.   Deduce the blossoms for the following functions:

     A. $5u^3 + u^2$.

     B. $\mathbf{b}u^2 + 2$.

3.   Do other blossom values have meaning apart from **a...a**, **0...0** **1...1**, etc.? For example, what is the meaning of **1,2,3** or **2.5,6, 10**?

The Power of the Blossom Form

Blossoms are very powerful. Once the principle is understood, methods may be generated to evaluate the Bézier curve, prove properties, define and evaluate B-spline curves, convert between B-spline and Bézier form, and much more.

The following two sections are intended for those who want more practice with blossoms. The material proves some new and some old things about Bézier curves by using blossoms. For example, one thing shown is that Bézier control points always have the form

$$\mathbf{b}_i = 0...01...i \text{ (there are i ones)}.$$

The Bézier Curve in Blossom Form

Using the three properties of blossoms previously described, the following can be observed

For the blossom $p(u_1, u_2, ..., u_N)$:

$$
\begin{aligned}
p(u,u,...,u) &= p((1-u) \cdot 0 + u \cdot 1, u, ..., u) \\
&= (1-u)p(0,u,...,u) + up(1,u,...,u) \\
&= (1-u)^2 p(0,0,u,...,u) + 2(1-u)up(0,1,u,...,u) + u^2 p(1,1,u,...,u) \\
&\quad \cdot \\
&\quad \cdot \\
&= (1-u)^N p(0,...,0) + N(1-u)^{N-1}up(0,...,0,1) + ... \\
&\quad + N(1-u)^{N-1}p(0,1,...,1) + u^N p(1,...,1).
\end{aligned}
$$

The point $p(u, u, ..., u)$ is on the curve $P(u)$ by the diagonal property. In the first equation, the first u in the argument list is written as an affine combination: $u = (1-u).0 + u.1$.

In the second line, the polynomial is factored by multiaffinity.

These steps are repeated for the next u in the argument list, and the terms are combined using the symmetry property to arrive at the third line. Continuing in this manner, the argument list is exhausted.

The polynomial, as seen in the last line, is a summation of coefficients, written as blossoms, multiplied by the *Bernstein basis polynomials*.[5] This polynomial is a Bézier curve of degree N. This can already be seen to be emerging in the third equation; the polynomials in each term are quadratic Bernstein polynomials.

The coefficients, or control points, are blossoms evaluated with only zeros and ones, so the blossoms p(0, 0,..., 1, 1) are then the Bézier control points, that is,

$$\mathbf{b}_i = p(0,\ldots,0,1,\ldots,1);$$

There are i ones in the blossom. This control point is the blossom evaluated at (N − i) zeros and i ones; the order does not matter.

Subdivision of the Bézier Curve Using Blossoms

- To subdivide a Bézier curve using blossoms, first let [s,t] be an arbitrary interval. Now, what are the Bézier control points over the interval [s,t]?

- Write the point on the curve at which subdivision is desired as

  $$p((1-u)\cdot s + u\cdot t,\ldots,(1-u)\cdot s + u\cdot t).$$

  The diagonal property ensures that the point is on the curve.

- Proceeding as before with the Bézier blossom description, with zeros becoming s, and ones becoming t,

  $$\mathbf{b}_i = p(s,\ldots,s,t,\ldots,t). \tag{5.4}$$

  There are i t's in this blossom. This is the ith Bézier control point over the interval [s,t].

Hence, if there were a method to evaluate the blossom of a polynomial, it could easily reparameterize over any interval. Specifically, it could be reparameterized over the interval [s,t] = [0,a] or [a,1]. This is equivalent to subdividing the Bézier curve at a parameter value a.

---

[5] Recall that the Bernstein basis polynomials are given by

$$B_i^n(t) = \frac{n!}{i!(n-i)!}(1-t)^{n-i}t^i.$$

Evaluating a Blossom from Bézier Control Points

Suppose that a set of Bézier control points is given. What is the point given by the blossom at $\mathbf{u}_1...\mathbf{u}_n$? The blossom properties lead to an algorithm that evaluates the blossom. It has the familiar form of iterated linear interpolation.

The EvalBlossom Algorithm

Use the property

$$p(0,\ldots,0,u_i,1,\ldots,1) = (1-u_i)p(0,\ldots,0,0,1,\ldots,1) + u_i p(0,\ldots,0,1,1,\ldots,1).$$

As with the de Casteljau algorithm, let the control points be the base of a systolic array. Then generate the points, row by row, in the array using linear interpolation. The final value is the blossom value. The difference in this algorithm is that the linear interpolation value changes for each row. It is $\mathbf{u}_N$ in the top row, $\mathbf{u}_{N-1}$ in the second, and so forth:

In this iterative procedure, the single element on the bottom row is the desired blossom value. The array provides a schematic for evaluating a blossom. The formal algorithm, called EvalBlossom, is as follows:

EvalBlossom($\mathbf{b}[0]$, ..., $\mathbf{b}[d]$, $u[1]$, ..., $u[d]$)

```
for i = 1 to d do
    for j = 0 to (d – i) do
        b[j] = (1 – u[i]) b[j] + u[i] b[j + 1]
    end
end
return b[0]
```

If $u = u[0] = u[1] = \ldots = u[N]$, then EvalBlossom is exactly the same as the de Casteljau algorithm for evaluating a Bézier curve at a parameter value u.

EvalBlossomProg: A General Blossom Algorithm

The de Casteljau algorithm generalizes to the EvalBlossom procedure. This assumes a [0, 1] range of curve parameterization, which may be a limitation in some circumstances. If EvalBlossom is extended to handle an arbitrary blossom parameterization, the result is the generalization known as EvalBlossomProg.

The algorithm is given by

EvalBlossomProg($\mathbf{b}[i]$, . . ., $\mathbf{b}[i + d]$, $u[1]$, . . ., $u[d]$, $t[i]$, . . ., $t[i + 2d – 1]$)

```
for k = 0 to (d – 1) do
    for j = 0 to (d – k – 1) do
        Beta = (u[k + 1] – t[i + k + j]) / (t[i + d + j] – t[i + k + j])
        Alpha = 1 – Beta
        b[j] = Alpha b[j] + Beta b[j + 1]
    end
end
return b[0]
```

In this algorithm b[i] are the de Boor points, which will be discussed in depth in Topic 6, "The B-Spline Curve." t[i] are the blossom parameterization values.

Illustration of the Cubic Blossom

The following figure shows the variation of the blossom arguments with the resulting values computed by EvalBlossomProg:

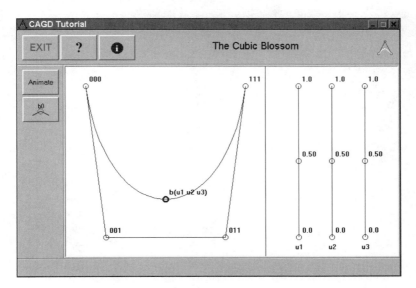

In the next figure, the blossom values are set to produce a point away from the Bézier curve:

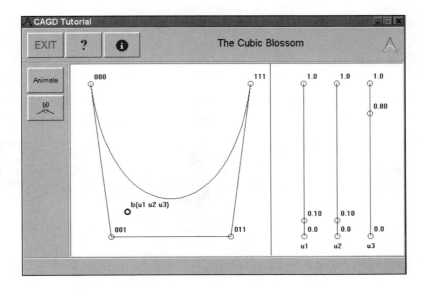

Finally, the same blossom values are used, but in a different sequence. The resulting point has not changed.

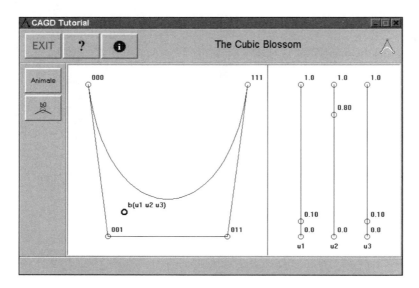

The question arises: Why determine any blossom value that is not on the curve, that is, not **aaa**? One example comes from the *reparameterization*[6] of the curve. Another way to reparameterize the curve is to use EvalBlossomProg. A Bézier curve is conventionally parameterized with a parameter in the range from 0 to 1. Now, what if another segment of the curve with parameter values from 2 to 3 were sought in terms of the Bézier control points?

For the cubic Bézier curve, the new control points will have the form **222**, **223**, **233**, and **333**. The first and last points are, of course, on the curve and are derived from de Casteljau's algorithm, but the others require the more general EvalBlossomProg.

[6] While it is convenient to parameterize curves in the interval [0, 1], there is nothing unique about this range. The same curve may be parameterized in the interval [−2, 2] if the blossom values are selected appropriately.

The following figure shows a parameter region from −2 to +2, with the control points computed by EvalBlossomProg:

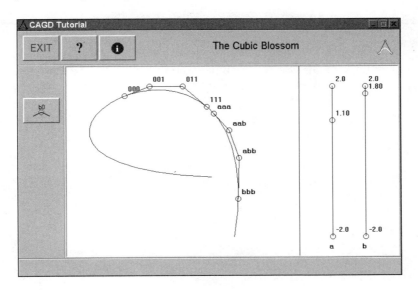

Now, using a different parameter range:

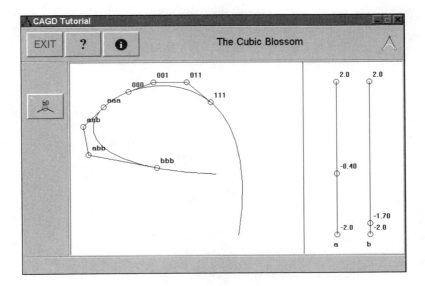

More importantly than reparameterization, blossoming gives the facility to define a new curve: the B-spline. This is fully covered in Topic 6, "The B-Spline Curve."

WHAT HAS BEEN ACCOMPLISHED IN THIS TOPIC

A strong base of knowledge concerning the blossom form has been built. This has allowed the investigation of the Bézier curve more deeply and will motivate the development of B-spline curves in Topic 6.

The B-Spline Curve

Introduction

The discussion of B-spline curves begins by considering a Bézier curve in blossom form.

In the following figure, a Bézier curve has control points **222**, **223**, **233**, and **333** in the parameter interval 2 to 3. Also shown are the blossom points **012**, **123**, **234**, and **345**.

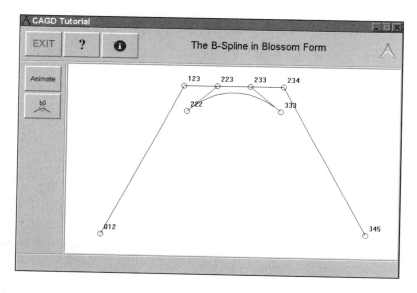

The next figure shows a new Bézier curve obtained by variation of the Bézier control points. Note how dramatically the blossom points **012**, **123**, **234**, and **345** respond to small changes in the original control points.

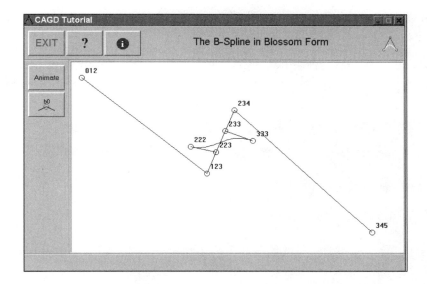

The additional points are computed with the *EvalBlossomProg*[1] routine, which was introduced in the last topic on blossoms. The new points **012**, **123**, **234**, and **345** are called the *de Boor*[2] points. When a curve is given by these points (instead of, for example, the Bézier control points), it is called a *B-spline curve*.[3]

[1] Recall the EvalBlossomProg procedure:

```
EvalBlossomProg(b[i], . . ., b[i + d], u[1], . . ., u[d], t[i], . . ., t[i + 2d − 1])

for k = 0 to (d − 1) do
    for j = 0 to (d − k − 1) do
        Beta = (u[k + 1] − t[i + k + j]) / (t[i + d + j] − t[i + k + j])
        Alpha = 1 − Beta
        b[j] = Alpha b[j] + Beta b[j + 1]
    end
end
return b[0]
```

[2] Carl de Boor, an American mathematician, developed the special case of EvalBlossomProg when the u(i) parameters are equal. It evaluates a B-spline.

[3] A spline was originally a strip made of wood or metal that is used to create a smooth curve through a set of points. This was the original method for creating smooth curves.

Superficially it seems that the Bézier form of the curve is better; it interpolates the endpoints, has endpoint tangents, and more closely approximates the control polygon. The advantage of B-spline curves comes when another blossom point is added at an arbitrary point in space: **456**. This point, when taken with **123**, **234**, and **345**, defines a new B-spline curve segment that runs from parameter value 3 to 4, as shown in the following figure:

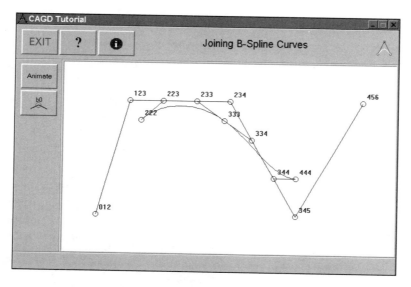

If the de Boor points are changed, the two curve segments retain their continuity:

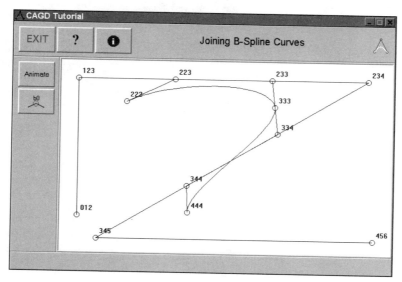

Notice that the two curve segments join smoothly without special effort. This is the strength and beauty of B-spline curves. In the cubic case they automatically join with C_2 *continuity*,[4] so long as the curve is not degenerate.

The following figure begins with a cubic B-spline curve, and then additional control points are added:

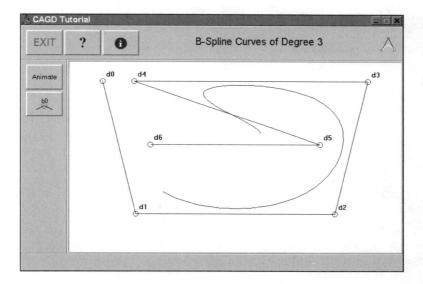

The power of B-spline curves is that one can create with ease a very complex curve that is smoothly connected. They are formed from sequential shifts: **012**, then **123**, then **234**. This is true for B-spline curves of any degree. Points **012**, . . . , **345** can be computed from EvalBlossomProg with **222**, . . . , **333** as input. De Boor point **456** does not come from these input points; rather, it was arbitrarily added. It actually belongs with a different curve, the second curve segment. EvalBlossomProg can also compute a point **456**; this is, of course, different from the point that was added.

What is needed is a method to evaluate the curves' Bézier control points, given the B-spline points. This is not hard when recalling the blossom properties; affine replacement still works, and **aaa** is still on the curve.

These ideas may be used to derive the de Boor algorithm for evaluating B-splines.

[4] Recall C_2 continuity: This means that the second derivatives of the curves are continuous.

The de Boor Algorithm

Start with the original set of de Boor points and find the point **2.5, 2.5, 2.5**, which is in the curve between parameter values 2 and 3.

Here is the starting set of de Boor points:

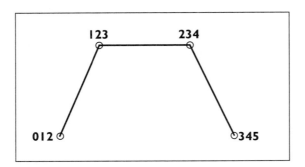

Begin with the first leg of the curve (**012** to **123**). The digits **1** and **2** are common; **0** changes to **3** as we progress along the curve.

Where is **1, 2, 2.5** in this progression? It is linearly interpolated along the line; it is 2.5/3 in affine distance along the polygon leg.

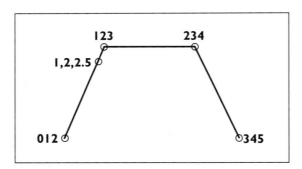

Similarly, **2, 2.5, 3** is found on the second leg, and **2.5, 3, 4** on the last leg.

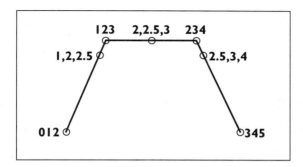

The replacement is repeated to find **2, 2.5, 2.5** (as **1** goes to **3**) and **2.5, 2.5, 3** (as **2** goes to **3**).

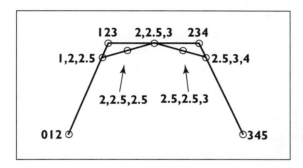

The final step yields **2.5, 2.5, 2.5**, a point on the curve.

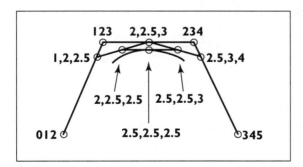

This process may be described as a systolic array.

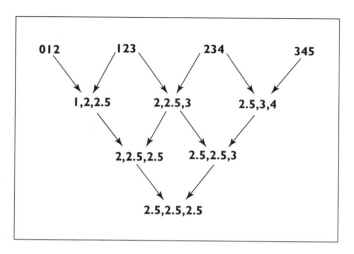

The condition to derive the point **1, 2, 2.5** is

$$\mathbf{1,2,2.5} = \frac{(2.5 - 0)}{(3 - 0)} \ \mathbf{1,2,3} + \frac{(3 - 2.5)}{(3 - 0)} \ \mathbf{0,1,2}.$$

As an exercise, be sure you are able to derive the other blossom points. If a parameter t is used instead of 2.5, then the condition above becomes

$$\mathbf{1,2,t} = \frac{(t - 0)}{(3 - 0)} \ \mathbf{1,2,3} + \frac{(3 - t)}{(3 - 0)} \ \mathbf{0,1,2}.$$

For a different interval, starting at the parameter value i, the condition is

$$\mathbf{i + 1, i + 2, t} = \frac{(t - i)}{(i + 3 - i)} \ \mathbf{i + 1, i + 2, i + 3} + \frac{(i + 3 - t)}{(i + 3 - i)} \ \mathbf{i, i + 1, i + 2}.$$

Finally, change the degree to n:

$$\mathbf{i + 1, i + 2, t} = \frac{(t - i)}{n} \ \mathbf{i + 1, i + 2, i + 3} + \frac{(i + n - t)}{n} \ \mathbf{i, i + 1, i + 2}.$$

This is for a single step in the array. The formal de Boor algorithm is written as

$$\mathbf{d}_i^K = \frac{(u_{i+n-k} - u)}{(u_{i+n-k} - u_{i-1})} \ \mathbf{d}_{i-1}^{K-1} + \frac{(u - u_{i-1})}{(u_{i+n-k} - u_{i-1})} \ \mathbf{d}_i^{K-1}, \tag{6.1}$$

where the $\mathbf{d}_i^0$ are the de Boor points.

The u values are the parameter intervals; n is the degree of the curve.

This equation is the well-known de Boor algorithm. The de Boor points **d** are associated with the blossom counterparts. The location of each succeeding level of points is made clear by the blossoms.

Summary of B-Splines in Blossom Form

The EvalBlossomProg procedure, in its more general form, gives

■ a method to evaluate B-spline curves,

■ a reparameterization method for B-spline curves (this also permits *subdivision*[5] of the curve),

■ a method to transform between B-spline curve segments and Bézier curves.

So far, only cubic B-spline curves have been discussed. In the following figures, B-splines of degree 2, 3, and 4 are shown.

First, a quadratic B-spline:

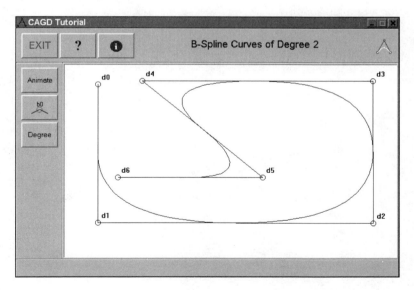

---

[5]   Subdivision is the process, usually through reparameterization, of separating a single curve segment into two parts.

Next, a cubic B-spline:

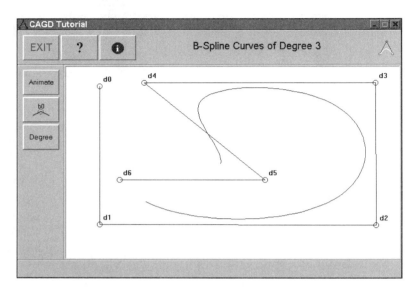

Finally, a quartic B-spline:

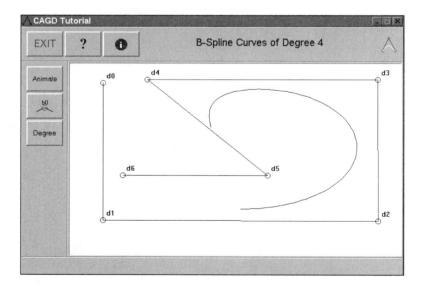

The B-spline control points in blossom form reveal much about the curve segment:

- The number of digits equals the degree (**012** is a control point for a cubic curve).

- There are sequential shifts of adjacent digits (**012, 123, 234,...**).

- The last digit of the first point and the first digit of the last point give the valid parameterization interval for the curve segment. In the cubic example, this interval is in the range 2...3.

- Adding one new point to the existing set gives another segment of the B-spline curve. This new segment typically joins the existing curve with degree n − 1 continuity.

EvalBlossomProg

Topic 5, "Blossoms," discussed how the de Casteljau algorithm generalizes to the EvalBlossom procedure. Does this analog hold for the de Boor algorithm? If de Boor's algorithm is evaluated with different parameter values at each level of iteration (exactly as in EvalBlossom), it can be shown that the appropriate blossom values are produced from the de Boor points. The generalization is known as EvalBlossomProg.

Recall this progression from the topic on blossoms. The top line of the figure contains the Bézier control points of the curve.

Also, recall that the algorithm is given by

EvalBlossomProg(**b**[i], . . ., **b**[i + d], u[1], . . ., u[d], t[i], . . ., t[i + 2d −1])

```
for k = 0 to (d − 1) do
    for j = 0 to (d − k − 1) do
        Beta = (u[k + 1] − t[i + k + j]) / (t[i + d + j] − t[i + k + j])
        Alpha = 1 − Beta
        b[j] = Alpha b[j] + Beta b[j + 1]
    end
end
return b[0]
```

In this algorithm the **b**[i] are the de Boor points. The t[i] are the blossom parameterization values for the B-spline, commonly known as *knots*.[6]

What can be done with this algorithm? Any blossom value can be generated from the de Boor points. In particular, the Bézier control points may be needed, so that B-spline curves may be converted to Bézier curves.

EXERCISES

1. Given the set of points {**012**, **123**, **234**, **345**}, construct the equivalent Bézier control points {**222**, **223**, **233**, **333**}.

2. Why were the points **000** and **111** not sought, to give a parameterization interval of 0 to 1? What significance to the B-spline do these points have?

[6]   EvalBlossomProg has introduced new quantities called knots. Since the B-spline uses fewer control points to define curve segments, there are clearly some degrees of freedom available for definition. These are the knots. Their geometric significance will become more apparent after the discussion on nonuniform B-spline curves.

Periodic B-Splines

If the first n and last n control points are made to coincide, then the curve's endpoints will match and it will form a closed curve. This is called a *periodic B-spline*. As before, each segment connects with its neighbors with degree n − 1 continuity. In the figure, d_0 and d_6 are coincident.

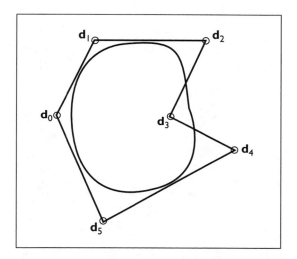

Nonuniform B-Splines

Thus far, the blossom arguments have been integers. There is no particular reason for this, apart from clarity. The blossom arguments may be any real numbers and all the previous methods will still work. For instance, a Bézier curve may be parameterized over the interval [2.5, 3]. Or, the B-spline control points may be given as {**0,1,2.5; 1,2.5,3; 2.5,3,4; 3,4,5**}. The change that occurs is similar to that in changing the parameterization in Lagrange interpolation.

The following figure shows the original cubic B-spline curve with its de Boor points, using integer blossom values {**012, 123, 234, 345**}. The subsequent figure uses the same points but with a different parameterization.

First, the original parameterization:

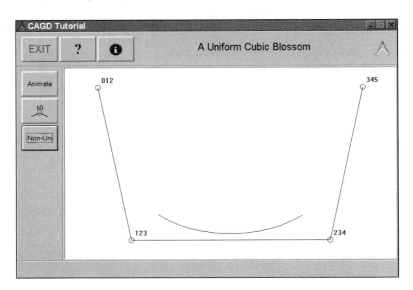

Now, the curve defined by the new parameterization:

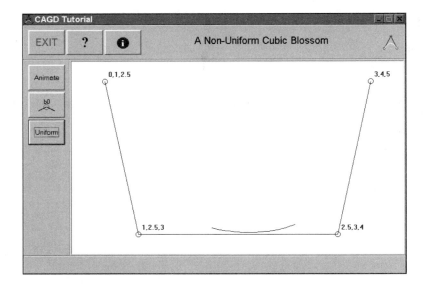

The blossoming principle still determines where to put points. They differ from the integer case because of different arguments. A B-spline curve with unequally spaced sequences is said to be *nonuniform*.[7] As with Lagrange interpolation, the arguments are called knots.

The following two figures demonstrate the effect of changing a curve's knot sequence. First, the original parameterization:

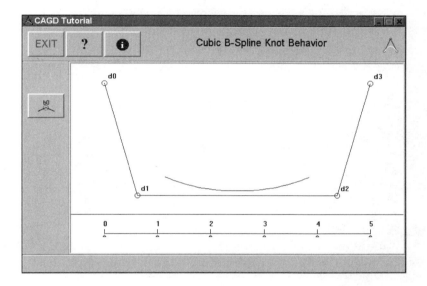

---

[7]   Nonuniform curves have a knot sequence in which the knots are   venly spaced.

Now, the new curve, with the knot sequence shown graphically beneath the curve:

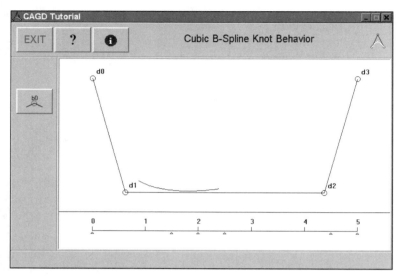

Basis Functions

A single B-spline curve segment is defined much like a Bézier curve. It looks like this:

$$\mathbf{d}(t) = \sum_{i=0}^{n} \mathbf{d}_i \, N_i(t), \tag{6.2}$$

where the **d** points are the de Boor points, the $N(t)$ are the basis functions, and n is the degree of the curve.

The basis functions used here are different from the Bernstein basis functions used by the Bézier curve.

The following figure shows the quadratic B-spline basis functions.

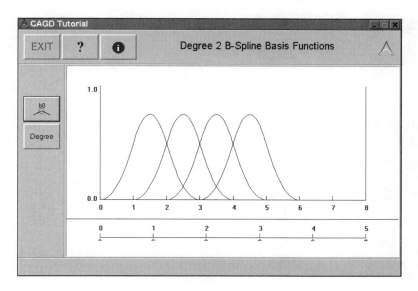

Now the cubic basis functions:

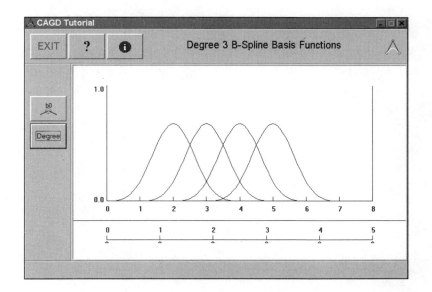

Now the quartic basis functions:

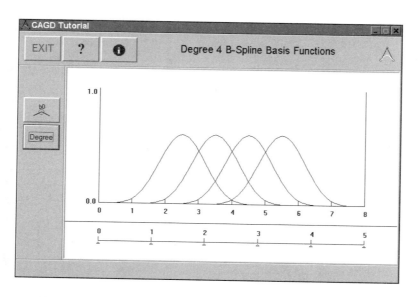

Finally, the last basis function figure shows the cubic B-spline basis functions for a nonuniform knot sequence. The knot sequence is shown beneath the basis functions.

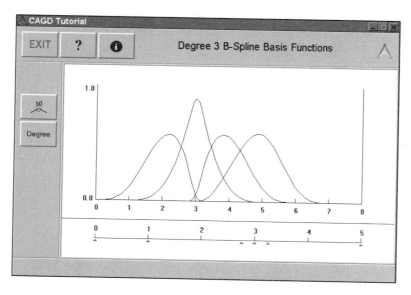

The basis functions for the B-spline curves are placed next to each other and overlap in a similar way to the control points. When they are drawn together, bell-shaped functions are generated that are zero outside a certain region of "support." It is also clear that they are simply translations of each other, for uniform knots.

It can be seen that (in the cubic case) for any parameter value t, only four basis functions are nonzero; thus, only four control points affect the curve at t. If a control point is moved, it influences only a limited portion of the curve.

This locality of influence is known as the *local support property*. In the same way as the Bernstein polynomials, the B-spline basis functions conform to the partition of unity:

$$\sum N_i(t) = 1.$$

This is used to prove that any point on the curve is a convex combination of the de Boor points; that is, it must be in the convex hull of the control points associated with the nonzero basis functions.

General Basis Functions

The basis functions considered so far have been cubic or of lower degree. Schoenberg first introduced the B-spline in 1949. He defined the basis functions using *integral convolution*[8] (the "B" in B-spline stands for "basis"). Higher degree basis functions are given by convolving multiple basis functions of one degree lower.

Linear basis functions are just "tents" as shown below. When convolved together, they make piecewise parabolic "bell" curves.

[8]   The convolution of f and g is given by
$$F(t) = \int f(x - t)g(x)dx.$$

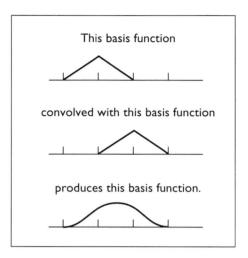

The tent basis function (which has a degree of one) is nonzero over two intervals, the parabola is nonzero over three intervals, and so forth. This gives the region of influence for different degree B-spline control points. Each convolution results in higher order continuity between segments of the basis function.

When the de Boor points are weighted by these basis functions, the B-spline curve results:

$$\mathbf{d}(t) = \sum_{i=0}^{n} \mathbf{d}_i N_i(t). \tag{6.3}$$

Instead of integrating to evaluate the basis functions, a recursive formula has been derived:

$$N_i^n = \frac{(u - u_{i-1})}{(u_{i+n-1} - u_{i-1})} N_i^{n-1}(u) + \frac{(u_{i+n} - u)}{(u_{i+n} - u_i)} N_{i+1}^{n-1}(u), \tag{6.4}$$

where

$$N_i^0(u) = \begin{cases} 1 \text{ if } u_{i-1} \le u \le u_i, \\ 0 \text{ otherwise.} \end{cases}$$

The terms in u represent the knot sequence, the spans over which the de Boor points influence the B-spline.

This recursive form is seldom used. The best way to evaluate a B-spline curve is to use the de Boor algorithm or the EvalBlossomProg algorithm.

Experiment with the B-Spline Curve

The following figures use the EvalBlossomProg routine to compute arbitrary blossom points, including (but not limited to) the B-spline curve.

First, note how the point **2.5**, **2.5**, **2.5** lies at the center of the B-spline:

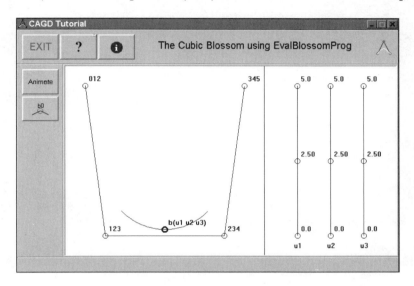

The following figure demonstrates the use of the blossom point **222** as an endpoint of the B-spline:

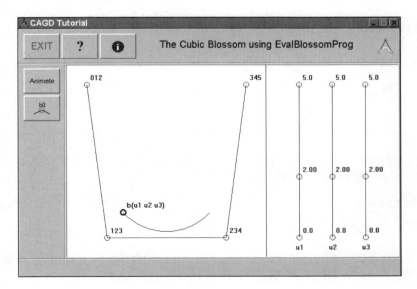

The following figure shows how blossom values outside the convex hull of the de Boor points are possible:

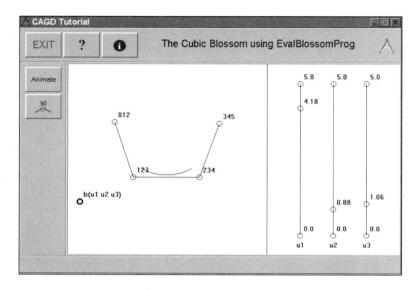

Knot Insertion

A Bézier curve can be subdivided into two curves that together duplicate the original. This important operation is the basis for many routines for evaluating curves. The analog for B-splines is an operation called *knot insertion*. It amounts to creating a new knot sequence with an extra coincident knot that is equivalent to subdividing a B-spline curve into two.

From the point of view of the blossom form, this means generating a new set of blossom points with one new point and there discovering the blossom value associated with the new argument. This is the key to the method, since the new value follows from the *blossoming principle*.[9]

---

[9]   The digit that differs between two blossoms is replaced with another value, giving the affine distance along the line segment for the new value.

Thus **axx** is found on the line segment between **bxx** and **cxx**, an affine distance given by

$$\frac{|\,\mathbf{bxx} - \mathbf{axx}\,|}{|\,\mathbf{cxx} - \mathbf{bxx}\,|}.$$

Consider a simple example. Let **01**, **12**, and **23** be de Boor points in blossom form in the following figure:

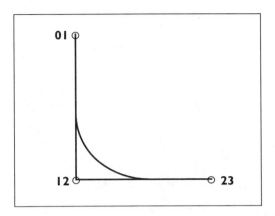

The valid parameter interval for the quadratic B-spline curve is $[1, 2]$ (from **11** to **22**). Now seek a new knot (for example, at a parameter value of 1.5) that can be used to divide the curve into two segments. These two segments match the original curve. To accomplish this, find

1. a new blossom sequence and
2. the corresponding blossom values.

The new sequence must be a shifted set of four values:

> {**0,1**; **1,1.5**; **1.5,2**; **2,3**}.

The blossom point **12** cannot be in this set, as it is not a shift of the knots. It is removed from the sequence. The new blossom values are easily derived from the now-familiar blossom principle. The blossom point **1,1.5** is on the line segment from **01** to **12**, an affine distance between **0** and **2**. Similarly **1.5,2** is on the line from **12** to **23**, an affine distance between **1** and **3**. This is illustrated in the following figure, which also shows the two new curve segments:

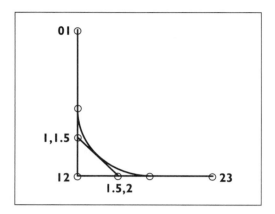

It should be clear that nonuniform B-splines are important in this process (if it isn't clear, look at the knot sequence for one of the curve segments: **0,1**; **1,1.5**; **1.5,2**). Even if the original points are uniform, the resulting knot insertion requires intermediate, unequally spaced values.

The two tasks generalize easily to any de Boor points in blossom form:

1. Create a new, sequentially shifted set of blossoms with the new knot.

2. Find the positions of the blossoms with the blossoming principle.

The first task admits only one obvious solution. It implies that some new knots are added (the same number as the degree of the curve), and some knots are removed (degree – 1 knots are removed).

Consider, for example, a nonuniform cubic B-spline:

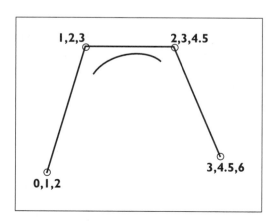

Inserting a knot at a parameter value of 2.4 divides the parameter range into two intervals. Putting the old sequence and the new sequence side by side often makes it clear which blossom values are deleted, which are new, and which remain the same:

Old Knots	*New Knots*
0,1,2	0,1,2
(1,2,3)	1,2,2.4
(2,3,4.5)	2,2.4,3
3,4.5,6	2.4,3,4.5
	3,4.5,6

The values in parentheses clearly do not belong since they do not contain **2.4** and they do not shift correctly. The italic values are the replacements.

WHAT HAS BEEN ACCOMPLISHED IN THIS TOPIC

The blossom principle has led naturally to B-splines, a type of curve used extensively in industry. This topic discussed the relationship between B-splines and Bézier curves, how the knot sequence modifies the curve, and how the characteristics of B-splines make them attractive as design tools.

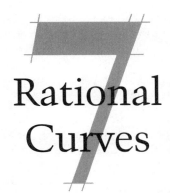

Rational
Curves

Introduction

A polynomial curve can exist in any dimension; it depends only on the number of dimensions used to describe the control points. Usually curves in CAGD are of two or three dimensions. The class of curves studied so far can be extended by considering projections of curves of a given dimension to a dimension lower by one. For example, a three-dimensional curve can be projected onto a two-dimensional plane.

The perspective projection is one familiar to programmers of computer graphics. Points in n-space are taken to a plane parallel to $n - 1$ axes, but displaced by a unit interval. A point is then projected along a straight line through the origin to the point of intersection with the plane.

The following figure illustrates the projection from $n = 3$ to $n = 2$:

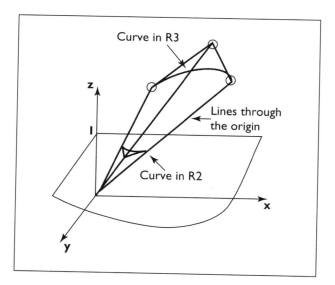

The idea generalizes for any n. For purposes of clarity, the projection from three dimensions to two dimensions will be used in this discussion.

Any point on the curve

$$f(t) = (x(t), y(t), z(t))$$

will project to the point:

$$r(t) = \left(\frac{x(t)}{z(t)}, \frac{y(t)}{z(t)} \right).$$

$$(7.1)$$

Points on the x, y plane where x and y are not zero are said to project to infinity.

The new, two-dimensional curve now has two coordinates found by dividing the x and y coordinates by the z coordinate. It is called a *rational curve.*[1] The set of rational curves includes all polynomial curves. This is seen by letting $z(t) = 1$. The set also includes all conic sections, that is, ellipses, parabolas, and hyperbolas. Except for the parabola, conic sections cannot be written as polynomial curves. In many applications exact conic sections are required. For instance, think of how often a circular arc is used in engineering. The support of conic sections was the main motive driving the development of rational curves. The rational curve also offers design flexibility.

The Two-Dimensional Rational Bézier Curve

A special notation is employed for writing the control points of a rational Bézier curve.

Start with a curve in three dimensions given by

$$\mathbf{f}(t) = \sum_{i=0}^{n} \begin{bmatrix} w_i x_i \\ w_i y_i \\ w_i \end{bmatrix} B_i(t).$$

Any control point in 3-space can be written by simply choosing the values of x and y appropriately; w is the z-coordinate.

From the projection above, the rational curve is

$$\mathbf{r}(t) = \left[\frac{\sum w_i x_i B_i(t)}{\sum w_i B_i(t)} \ , \ \frac{\sum w_i y_i B_i(t)}{\sum w_i B_i(t)} \right]. \tag{7.2}$$

The numerator and denominator always match in degree.

Now, let

$$\mathbf{b}_i = [x_i, y_i].$$

---

[1]　Rational curves are so named because they are written as a ratio. They are the quotient of two polynomials.

Now the rational Bézier curve may be described with more conventional notation:

$$\mathbf{r}(t) = \frac{\displaystyle\sum_{i=0}^{n} w_i \mathbf{b}_i B_i(t)}{\displaystyle\sum_{i=0}^{n} w_i B_i(t)} .$$ \hfill (7.3)

To define a rational Bézier curve, give a control polygon as before, and with each control point, associate a value w, called its *weight*.[2]

The following figures show a quadratic rational Bézier curve projection and its 2-space equivalent.

While observing these figures, notice what happens when the weight values are changed.

First, the curve with identical weights at each control point:

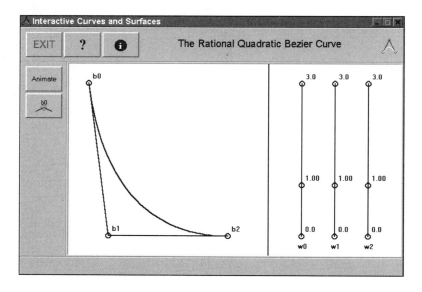

---

[2]   The weight w of a control point is a measure of the contribution the point makes to the final curve.

Now, set the weight $w_1 = 2.5$. The curve is "pulled" toward the control point with the greater weight.

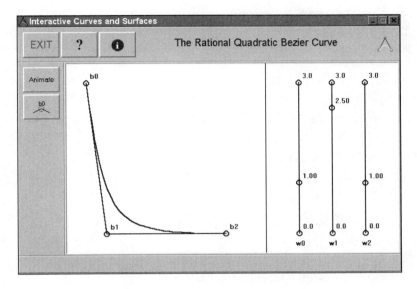

There is some redundancy in the choice of weights. The same curve is given by

$$w_0 = w_2 = 1; w_1 = 2$$

as by

$$w_0 = w_2 = k; w_1 = 2k.$$

The curve in 3-space simply scales without changing the projection. The redundancy can be eliminated by standardizing the quadratic curve so that

$$w_0 = w_2 = 1.$$

Given any set of weights, the formula for standardizing the curve is the following: Replace w_i with $\overline{w}_i$, where

$$\overline{w}_i = p^{2i} w_i$$

and

$$p = \sqrt{\frac{w_2}{w_0}}.$$

This replacement does not change the form of the curve. Finally, by dividing through by w_2, the standard form is obtained.

Finding the Conic Sections

From a rational quadratic Bézier curve in standard form, it is easy to obtain the conic sections. If $w_1 = 1$, then a parabola results. If $w_1 < 1$, then the curve is an ellipse. If $w_1 > 1$, then the curve is a hyperbola.

The case of the circle deserves special attention. Use the ellipse condition, $w_1 < 1$, but the control points **b** also play a role. The condition is as follows.

If α is the angle formed by $\mathbf{b}_0$, $\mathbf{b}_1$, and $\mathbf{b}_2$, then

$$w_1 = \cos\left(\frac{\alpha}{2}\right).$$

Because of the symmetry of the circle, the control points must also be configured symmetrically as an isosceles triangle. The following figures show what happens when $w_0 = w_2 = 1$.

The value of the intermediate weight may be varied to obtain a parabola, an ellipse, and a hyperbola.

First, set all three weights equal to 1, to obtain a parabola:

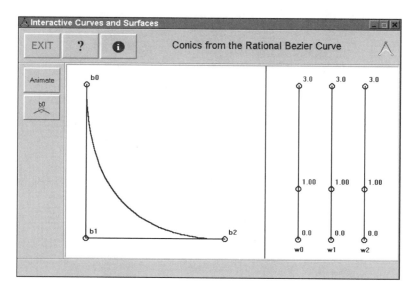

Now, set $w_1 = 0.5$, to obtain a portion of an ellipse:

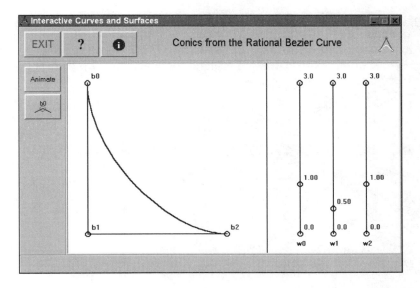

Now, set $w_1 = 2.5$, to obtain a hyperbola:

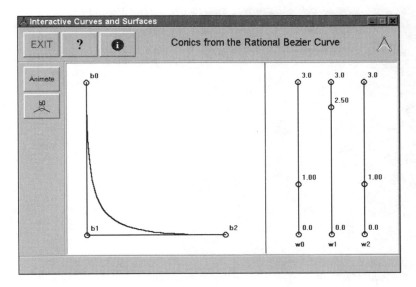

The General Rational Bézier Curve

As alluded to previously, the control points **b** may be of any dimension. Add one more coordinate, the weight, to define the curve in a higher dimensional space. This space is called the *projective space*. To obtain the rational curve, project the polynomial curve onto the hyperplane. Behavior and properties of the rational curve derive from this operation.

The following figures explore in detail the properties of the cubic rational Bézier curve. First, here is the curve with identical weights of unity:

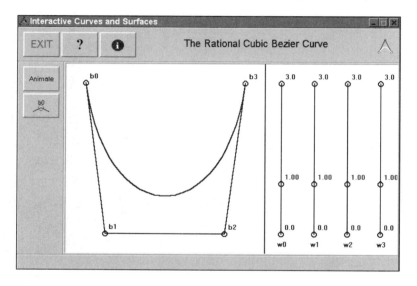

Now, set $w_1 = 2.8$. This pulls the curve toward $\mathbf{b}_1$:

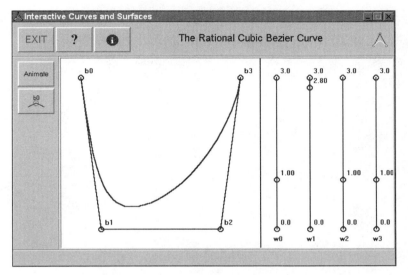

Next, set $w_1 = w_2 = 0.25$. This causes the curve to be pulled harder toward $\mathbf{b}_0$ and $\mathbf{b}_3$:

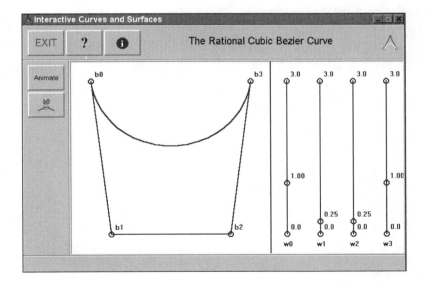

Finally, set all the weights equal to 0.25. The curve is identical to the original, with all weights set to 1:

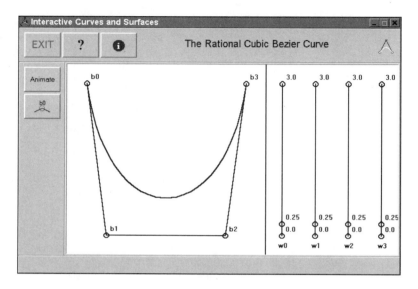

The first thing that becomes apparent when studying the general case of the rational Bézier curve is that the equation

$$\mathbf{r}(t) = \frac{\sum_{i=0}^{n} w_i \mathbf{b}_i B_i(t)}{\sum_{i=0}^{n} w_i B_i(t)}$$

can be rewritten as

$$\mathbf{r}(t) = \sum_{i=0}^{n} \mathbf{b}_i R_i(t) \ , \tag{7.4}$$

where

$$R_i(t) = \frac{w_i B_i(t)}{\sum_{j=0}^{n} w_j B_j(t)} \ . \tag{7.5}$$

Investigation of this newly defined set of basis functions reveals partition of unity, convex hull, and endpoint interpolation properties. The rational Bézier curve also has all the properties from the polynomial form, that is,

- affine invariance,

- tangent interpolation at endpoints,

- variation diminishing,

- linear precision.

The important de Casteljau algorithm can be applied to the rational curve by applying it in projective space. That is, the curve is evaluated in one dimension higher by de Casteljau and then the projection is performed. This involves the division by the weight coordinate. This procedure may also be used to subdivide the curve.

The only reservation to this approach is that the final divide may cause numerical instability. [Farin93] gives an alternative with greater numerical stability.

The weights of a rational curve can add some design flexibility. The movement of a control point moves any point on the curve in a parallel direction, as shown in the following figure:

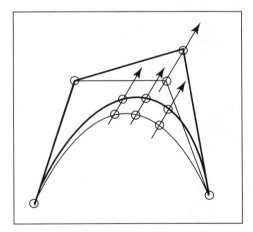

However, if only the weight is changed, not the control point, then the points on the curve move along a line toward the associated control point:

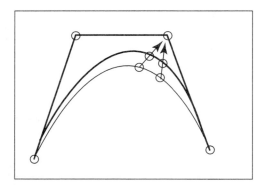

Besides the ability to handle conics and to gain design flexibility, the rational form allows freedom through the weights to solve certain other problems. Such problems include higher order interpolatory reparameterization without changing the curve shape, and curve fairing, or smoothing.

The following figures show two cases of the movement of points on the curve.

First, the original rational cubic Bézier curve with identical weights associated with each control point:

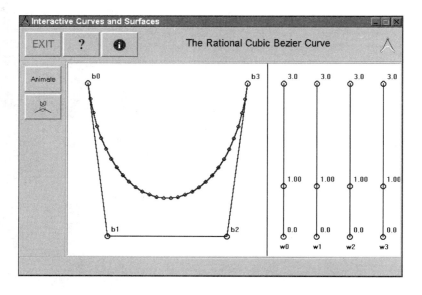

Now observe how points on the Bézier curve move when the weights are adjusted:

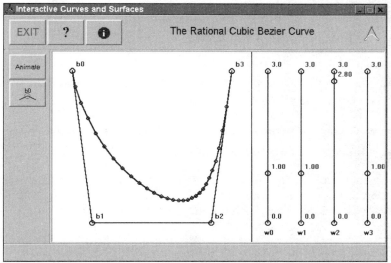

Rational B-Spline Curves

The rational B-spline curve is defined in direct analogy to the rational Bézier; it is a projection of the B-spline curve to a space of lower dimension. This makes obvious sense given that the B-spline curve can be converted to Bézier form. If this is done in projective space, then the rational B-spline curve and the rational Bézier curve can be converted into each other:

Projection space: Bézier $\leftrightarrow$ B-spline

                            $\downarrow$ $\downarrow$

                  Rational Bézier   Rational B-spline

The form of a rational B-spline curve is

$$\mathbf{f}(t) = \frac{\displaystyle\sum_{i=0}^{L+n-1} w_i \mathbf{d}_i N_i(u)}{\displaystyle\sum_{i=0}^{L+n-1} w_i N_i(u)} \, . \tag{7.6}$$

Here, the **d** are the de Boor points and N(u), the B-spline basis functions. L is the number of segments. As with the Bézier curve, the w values represent the weights associated with the de Boor points.

The most general form of a curve discussed thus far is the rational form of the nonuniform B-spline. It is called a NURBS (nonuniform rational B-spline). It is described by control (de Boor) points, a set of weights, and a knot sequence.

Operations and properties follow for the NURBS from the B-spline in the same way as seen for the rational Bézier curve.

WHAT HAS BEEN ACCOMPLISHED IN THIS TOPIC

Rational curves extend the capabilities of standard Bézier and B-spline curves, and permit conic sections to be realized. With the introduction of further degrees of freedom, the designer has a tool to solve additional problems.

Surfaces

Introduction to Surfaces

Imagine moving the set of control points of the Bézier curve in three dimensions. As they move in space, new curves are generated. If they are moved smoothly, then the curves formed create a surface, which may be thought of as a bundle of curves. If each of the control points is moved along a Bézier curve of its own, then a Bézier surface patch is created.

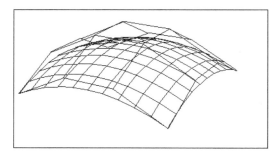

This can be described by changing the control points in the *Bézier formula*[1] into Bézier curves; thus a surface is defined by

$$s(u,v) = \sum_{i=0}^{n} b_i(u)B_i(v). \tag{8.1}$$

Notice there is one parameter for the control curves and one for the "swept" curve. It is convenient to write the control curves as Bézier curves that have the same degree as the original control curves. Given that the ith control curve has control points b_{ij}, then the surface given in equation 8.1 above can be written as

$$s(u,v) = \sum_{i=0}^{n} \left[\sum_{j=0}^{m} b_{ij} B_j(u) \right] B_i(v), \tag{8.2}$$

where m is the degree of the control curves.

---

[1] The equation for the standard Bézier curve is

$$f(t) = \sum_{i=0}^{n} b_i B_i^n(t).$$

Such a surface can be thought of as nesting one set of curves inside another. From this simple characteristic, many properties and operations for surfaces may be derived.

Simple algebra changes equation 8.2 above into

$$\mathbf{s}(u,v) = \sum_{i=0}^{n} \left[\sum_{j=0}^{m} \mathbf{b}_{ij} \, B_j(u) \right] B_i(v) = \sum_{i=0}^{n} \sum_{j=0}^{m} \mathbf{b}_{ij} B_i(u) B_j(v). \tag{8.3}$$

That is, even though one curve was swept along the other, there is no preferred direction. The surface patch could have been written as

$$\mathbf{s}(u,v) = \sum_{i=0}^{n} \mathbf{b}_j(v) B_j(u), \tag{8.4}$$

where

$$\mathbf{b}_j(v) = \sum_{i=0}^{n} \mathbf{b}_{ij} \, B_i(v). \tag{8.5}$$

The curve is simply swept in the other direction.

The set of control points forms a rectangular control mesh. A 3 by 3 (bicubic) control mesh is shown here:

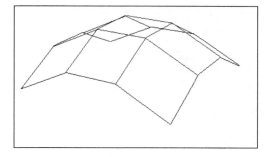

There are 16 control points in the bicubic control mesh. In general there will be (n + 1) by (m + 1) control points. By convention, the i index is associated with the u parameter, and the j index with the v parameter. Hence,

$\mathbf{b}_{i0}, \ i = 1 \ldots n$

gives the Bézier curve

$$\mathbf{b}(u,0) = \sum_{i=0}^{n} \mathbf{b}_{i0} B_i^n(u). \tag{8.6}$$

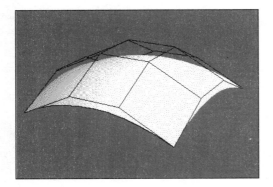

Each marginal set of control points defines a Bézier curve (the four border curves), and each of these curves is a boundary of the Bézier surface patch. Such a curve is shown at the forward edge of the patch in the preceding figure.

Properties of the Bézier Surface Patch

Many of the properties of the Bézier surface are derived directly from those of the Bézier curve, especially those curves that form the boundaries of the patch.

Endpoint Interpolation

The Bézier surface patch passes through all four corner control points. Formally, for the bicubic case,

$$\mathbf{b}(0,0) = \mathbf{b}_{00};\ \mathbf{b}(0,1) = \mathbf{b}_{03};\ \mathbf{b}(1,0) = \mathbf{b}_{30};\ \mathbf{b}(1,1) = \mathbf{b}_{33}.$$

Tangent Conditions

The four border curves of the Bézier surface patch are cotangent to the first and last segments of each border control polygon, at the first and last control points. The normal to the surface patch at each vertex may be found from the cross product of the tangents.

Convex Hull

The Bézier surface patch is contained in the convex hull of its control mesh for $0 \leq u \leq 1$ and $0 \leq v \leq 1$.

Affine Invariance

The Bézier surface patch is affinely invariant with respect to its control mesh. This means that any linear transformation or translation of the control mesh defines a new patch that is just the transformation or translation of the original patch.

Variation Diminishing

Although this is difficult to define for surfaces, the control mesh suggests the shape of the patch.

Planar Precision

The Bézier surface patch has planar precision: if all the points in the control mesh lie in a plane, the surface patch will lie in the same plane; if all the points in the control mesh form a straight line, the surface is also reduced to a line.

Evaluation of the Bézier Surface Patch

As with the properties described above, the evaluation of a Bézier surface patch can also be derived from the Bézier curve. To evaluate a point on the patch at parameter value (u, v), apply the *de Casteljau algorithm*[2] in a nested fashion similar to equation 8.3. That is, first evaluate the control curves in the u direction, which reduce to control points in the v direction. These points are again evaluated with de Casteljau's algorithm.

[2] De Casteljau's algorithm evaluates points on a Bézier curve by a process of recursive linear interpolation. At each successive level in the iteration, the algorithm converges to the curve.

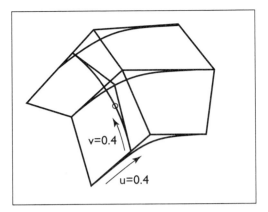

In the preceding figure, a point on a biquadratic Bézier surface patch is evaluated by first computing three points in u, then one point in v. There are nine points (3 by 3) in the control mesh.

As explained earlier, the order of u and v is not important: the same point is generated by evaluating in v first, and then in u.

Any other evaluation technique used for Bézier curves may be applied in a nested fashion to surfaces.

Subdivision of the Bézier Surface Patch

As with the Bézier curve, the de Casteljau algorithm can be applied to subdivide a Bézier surface patch. When a surface patch is subdivided, it yields four subpatches that share a corner at the (u, v) subdivision point.

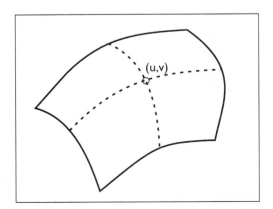

Recall that when a curve was subdivided, the new curve's control points appeared as the legs of a *systolic array*.[3] In the surface case, subdividing each row of the control mesh produces points of the systolic array for each.

Each point on each leg of every row's systolic array now becomes a control point for a columnar set. A biquadratic case is shown here:

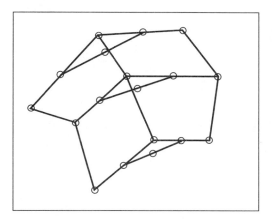

In this case, three points in each row produce five points after subdivision.

[3]   The systolic array

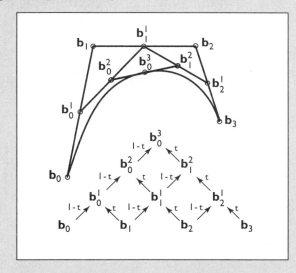

Now consider the points in columns, subdividing the columns with de Casteljau's algorithm. The points in the legs of their systolic arrays become the control points of the new subpatches. In the preceding example, rows with three control points produce five "leg" points, that is, five columns of three points. Each column then produces five control points; so, a 3 by 3 grid generates a 5 by 5 grid after subdivision:

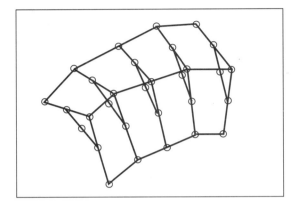

The control meshes of the four new patches are produced as follows:

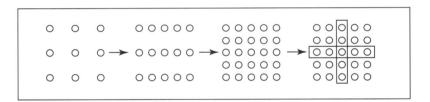

The central row and column of control points are shared by each 3 by 3 subpatch:

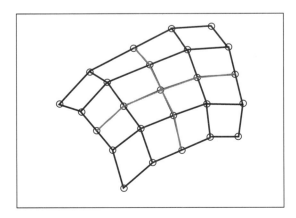

The order of the scheme does not matter. Columns may have been taken first, and then rows.

Subdivision is a basic operation of surfaces. Many "divide and conquer" algorithms are based on it. Imagine clipping a surface to a viewing window with the two properties of

- convex hull property

- subdivision

Hint: It is much easier to test the convex hull of a patch against a viewing window than the patch itself.[4]

Uniform B-Spline Surfaces

As with the Bézier surface, the B-spline surface is defined as a nested bundle of curves, thus yielding

$$s(u,v) = \sum_{i=0}^{L+n-1} \sum_{j=0}^{M+m-1} d_{ij} N_i(u) N_j(v), \tag{8.7}$$

where

- N_i are the familiar B-spline basis functions,

- n, m are the degrees of the B-splines,

- L, M are the number of segments, so there are L by M patches.

---

[4] Recursively perform the following:

- Test the convex hull of the patch against the viewing window; if clipping is necessary, then continue, else exit.

- Subdivide the patch at u = 0.5, v = 0.5; test the convex hulls of each subpatch against the viewing window.

- Render those patches that intersect the viewing window; ignore those patches outside the viewing window.

- Recurse, subdividing patches that still intersect the window.

- Continue until the patches are beneath a certain preset threshold.

All operations used for B-spline curves carry over to the surface via the nesting scheme, including knot insertion, de Boor's algorithm, and so on.

B-spline curves are especially convenient for obtaining continuity between polynomial segments. This convenience is even stronger in the case of B-spline surfaces:

■ C_{m-1}, C_{n-1} continuity is maintained between the subpatches.

■ B-splines define quilts of patches with corresponding design flexibility.

B-spline curves are more compact at representing a design than Bézier curves. This advantage is "squared" in the case of surfaces.

These advantages are tempered by the fact that operations are typically more efficient on Bézier curves. Conventional wisdom says that it is best to design and represent surfaces as B-splines, and then convert to Bézier form for operations.

The following figure shows a simple B-spline surface patch:

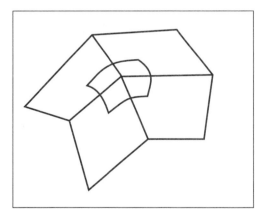

What Has Been Accomplished in This Topic

The majority of industrial design tasks require the creation of three-dimensional products. Bézier and B-spline surface patches supply the tools for such products.

This topic has introduced descriptions for these surface patches and given their advantages and behavior. Subdivision of the Bézier patch was also presented.

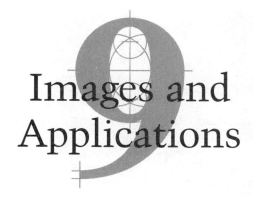

Images and Applications

IN THIS TOPIC, YOU WILL LEARN

- tools to evaluate the properties of a surface,
- how CAGD assists design of industrial products,
- uses of CAGD that are creative and artistic as well as functional.

Introduction

The best method of evaluating the properties of an object's surface, apart from actually manufacturing the object, is to visualize the object with a computer. This method is commonly applied for engineering, analysis, styling, marketing, and in the conceptual stages of a project. This topic presents examples of some of these applications.

Evaluating Surface Characteristics: Reflection Maps

Imagine a bank of parallel fluorescent tubes illuminating an object. The reflections of the lights flow across the surface and accurately indicate the continuity between surface patches. The following three figures demonstrate this method using two surface patches of different continuity across the boundary.

G_0 Continuity

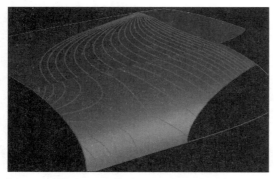

Courtesy of Parametric Technology Corp. © 1995
Data generated by Pro/CDRS

Here, the patches are connected with positional (G_0) continuity. The reflection lines indicate discontinuous jumps. The reflections trace the behavior of the surface normals, which are discontinuous at the join between the two patches.

G_1 Continuity

Courtesy of Parametric Technology Corp. © 1995
Data generated by Pro/CDRS

When the two patches meet with tangent (G_1) continuity, the reflection lines meet but kink at the patch boundary.

G_2 Continuity

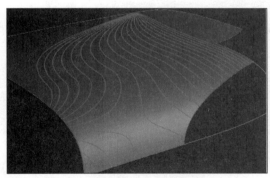

Courtesy of Parametric Technology Corp. © 1995
Data generated by Pro/CDRS

With higher orders of continuity (here, G_2), the reflection lines are smooth as they cross the patch boundary. This can be quite important in such fields as car design.

Evaluating Surface Characteristics: Hedgehog Display

Another way to view surface continuity and shape is through hedgehog display. Each "spine" of the hedgehog is a surface normal to the displayed object. The length of the normal varies with the curvature of the surface. Regions of higher curvature are shown by using longer surface normals. For this tool to be useful, the parametrization must be carefully chosen to give consistent surface normals on the different surface patches.

G_0 Continuity

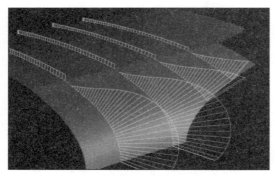

Courtesy of Parametric Technology Corp. © 1995
Data generated by Pro/CDRS

When the patches are connected with positional (G_0) continuity, the surface normals exhibit significant change in both size and direction at the patch boundary.

G_1 Continuity

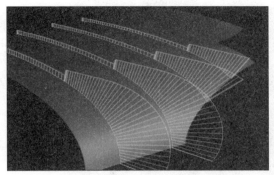

Courtesy of Parametric Technology Corp. © 1995
Data generated by Pro/CDRS

Where surface patches meet with tangent (G_1) continuity, the surface normals are parallel at the boundary but are not of equal length. This indicates that there is a discontinuity in curvature at the boundary.

G_2 Continuity

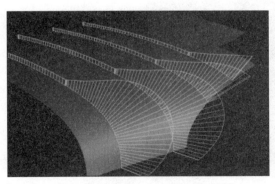

Courtesy of Parametric Technology Corp. © 1995
Data generated by Pro/CDRS

With G_2 continuity, the surface normals have equal length and direction across the boundary.

Faceting: The Display of Complex Surfaces

The display of complex surface patches often requires approximating the patches with polygonal facets. Graphics workstations usually accept triangular or quadrilateral facets, which are shaded and displayed by hardware. The resolution of the facets can be controlled to optimize the speed or quality of display.

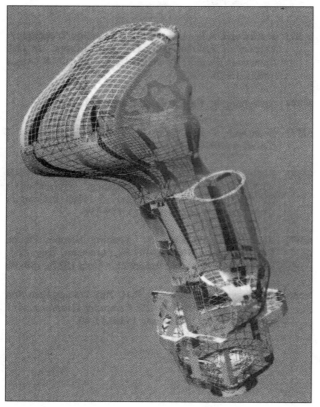

Alyn Rockwood

This image shows the facets of a joystick that will be used to display the part.

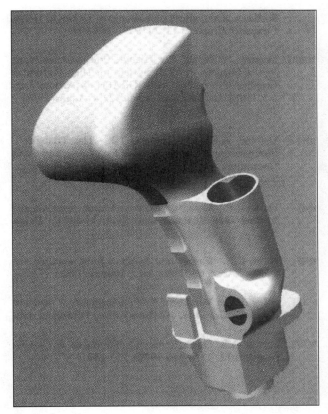

Alyn Rockwood

Here, the joystick is fully rendered using Gouraud shading, a standard graphics illumination model.

The Utah Teapot: Texturing and Bump Mapping

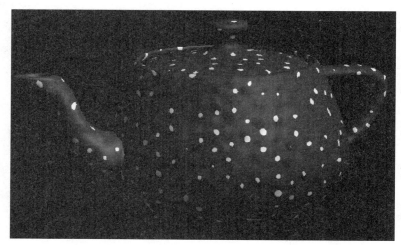

Peter Chambers

Several methods exist to apply texture to a surface by mapping color patterns onto the surface. The preceding figure shows the Utah teapot, a popular benchmark for surfaces.

The teapot is textured by a random polka-dot pattern. Bump mapping [Blinn78] perturbs the normal of the surface so that the object appears dimpled when illuminated by standard graphics routines.

Texturing methods greatly extend the application domain for surfaces in computer graphics and animation.

The Utah Teapot Rendered by Contouring

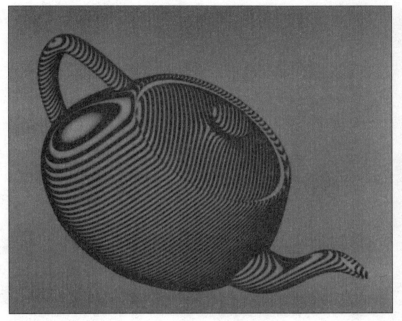

Alyn Rockwood

This time the Utah teapot is rendered by contouring. This method is also known as "water levels" or "breadslicing." It indicates a set of parallel plane cuts through the surface. Contouring can reveal surface characteristics that are difficult to discern with natural illumination. For example, it indicates which parts of the surface are at the same level, given an orientation of the cutting plane with respect to the object.

Flat areas and singular regions (saddle points and extrema) also become readily evident. Such areas in the teapot are seen on the handle, the spout, the body near the handle, and on the knob of the lid.

Simple Display and Illumination of a Turbine Blade

Alyn Rockwood

A simple illumination model, simulating just diffuse lighting together with highlights, is less than realistic in effect. However, it reveals essential aspects of the object as clearly as a highly detailed rendering.

Transparent surfaces permit viewing of underlying surfaces while maintaining the relationship of the outer surface.

Image Gallery

The following images show the diversity and effectiveness of modeling with surfaces, especially with good display routines.

Automobile Front End

Courtesy of Parametric Technology Corp. © 1995
Data generated by Lan Zaback, Pro/CDRS, rendered in Pro/PHOTORENDER

The combination of CAGD and high-quality rendering algorithms produces considerable realism, allowing for aesthetic consideration of an object.

Ski Boot

Courtesy of Intermountain Design, Inc.
Data generated by Pro/CDRS, rendered in Pro/PHOTORENDER
© 1995, Intermountain Design, Inc.

Realistic display techniques allow for product evaluation, marketing, and other commercially useful applications.

Machine Gear

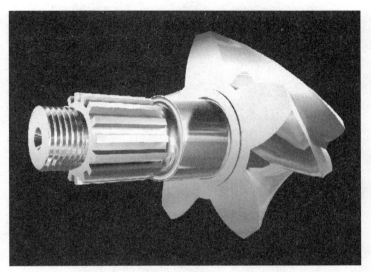

© 1994 Autodesk, Inc. Reprinted with permission.
From the Second Annual Autodesk International Image and Animation Contest, 1994.
Submitted by John W. Barton, Jr.

This image demonstrates the capability of CAGD for effectively creating the complex curves of a precision component.

Bicycle Wheel

© 1994 Autodesk, Inc. Reprinted with permission.
From the Second Annual Autodesk International Image and Animation Contest, 1994.
Submitted by Andrew Rodriquez.

Note the attention to detail in the modeling.

Still Life

From the Second Annual Autodesk International Image and Animation Contest, 1994.
Submitted by Hyun-Deok Shim.

This image shows a variety of realistic surface textures and uses a very effective illumination model.

WHAT HAS BEEN ACCOMPLISHED IN THIS TOPIC

The use of interactive, visual tools is commonplace in CAGD. This topic has shown how reflection maps and the hedgehog display assist designers in the evaluation of a surface's characteristics, as examples of visual tools. Further, some examples of objects created with commercial CAGD environments were included.

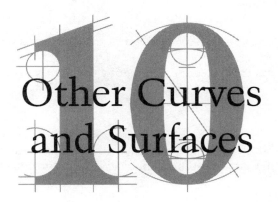

Other Curves and Surfaces

IN THIS TOPIC, YOU WILL LEARN ABOUT OTHER USEFUL CURVES AND SURFACES, INCLUDING

- the Gregory patch,
- implicit curves and surfaces,
- nonrectangular patches.

Those who have mastered the material so far should have the basic understanding and skills for designing with curves and surfaces. A vast field of further inquiry is available to those who wish to explore the subject in greater depth.[1]

This topic gives a brief overview of some concepts not yet covered, with pointers to where more information can be found. CAGD is a very active and broad research area, and new research is appearing constantly.

Other Curves

The systolic array seen before as the de Casteljau and de Boor algorithms can be generalized by computing each value from previous ones in the array as follows:

$$L(t)\mathbf{b}_i^k \ \ldots\ldots R(t)\mathbf{b}_i^k$$
$$\downarrow$$
$$\mathbf{b}_i^{k+1}$$

The "left" and "right" functions, L and R, are linear functions of some parameter t. The de Casteljau algorithm makes a simple assignment for L and R, specifically, $1 - t$ and t, where $0 < t < 1$.

Other choices of L and R generate different curves. What if $L(t) = 2t - 1$ and $R(t) = t + 10$? It would create a new polynomial curve type. It may not be useful in design, but it is new.

It should be clear that there are infinitely many curve definitions. All of them could be rationalized in the same fashion as rational Bézier or B-spline. [Goldman88] has shown that L and R can be related to choosing balls from an urn and that the curve at t is a weighted probability distribution based on an "urn" model.

The utility of any curve is more likely to be understood from its basis functions that each systolic array produces. Earlier topics have discussed how Bézier, Lagrange, Hermite, and B-spline basis functions define the properties of a curve.

---

[1]   Some good general texts and reference articles include [Barnhill74], [Bartels87], [Boehm84], [deBoor78], [Farin93], [Faux79], [Foley92], [Hoschek89], and [Hoffmann89].

In the cubic Catmull-Rom spline [Catmull & Rom74], the tangent at a control point c_i is parallel to the chord from c_{i-1} to c_{i+1}, as shown here:

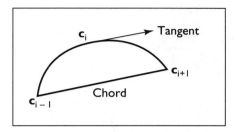

This spline was discovered and used independently in the FMILL system for automatic milling [Faux79].

In his thesis, Catmull also developed a polynomial basis for curves that had the main benefit that subdivision at the midpoint was computationally efficient [Catmull74].

Higher-order Hermite curves that have degree = $2k + 1$ for $k > 1$ (odd numbers) are other examples of curves with different bases [Farin93]. These curves determine curvature as well as tangent direction at the boundaries.

Nielson's nu spline [Nielson86] has shaping controls for tightening or flattening curves as shown in the following figure. The ν parameter is chosen so that it adjusts the tangents of the Hermite form by a factor ν so that the curve minimizes a function:

$$\int_{u_0}^{u_L} [x''(t)]^2 dt + \sum \nu_i [m_i]^2, \tag{10.1}$$

where m_i is the ith tangent.

The first part of the function gives an approximation to minimum curvature for the curve $x(t)$. Therefore the curve has a generally pleasing appearance. As the ν_i tend to infinity, the lengths of the tangents m_i must go to zero. This yields a tighter fit of the curve at the control points.

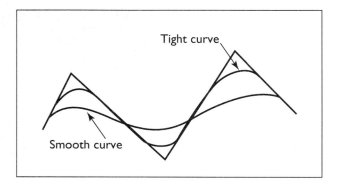

Boehm extended the B-spline to allow definition of another parameter γ at each control point, described in [Farin93]. Intuitively, the Gamma spline allowed the designer to draw the curve closer to the point with a sharper bend in much the same way that a weight operates in rational curves or the nu operates in the v spline. However, the Gamma spline is polynomial like the v spline.

In an independent but related effort, [Barsky81] devised a method that amounted to deforming the v spline. He rescaled each interval of the knot sequence to unit length, which may allow discontinuities of tangent. The rescaling parameters β_i can be linked to create global shaping factors that sharpen or flatten the curve, or can be adjusted individually.

Nonpolynomial curves have been defined using, for example, the exponential functions to define a basis. Rational Gaussian curves (RaGs) [Goshtasby93] use the rational form of the exponential functions to achieve a convex hull property with smooth shapes.

Other Surfaces

Clearly the curve forms discussed above could define tensor product surfaces in the same manner as before, that is, by multiplying terms of two curves. Recall that it was most convenient to think of sweeping one curve into a surface by making control points into "control curves." Algebra then showed that the resulting nesting was arbitrary (see Topic 8, "Surfaces"). There are, however, many surface forms that are not tensor products.

One of the earliest and still most important non-tensor product surfaces is the Coons patch, named after Steven Coons [Coons64], [Forrest72], and [Barnhill82]. It solves the problem of defining a surface between a given network of parametric curves. These curves do not have to be of the same type. It is possible to mix RaGs, v splines, and trigonometric curves if desired, as long as they are given parametrically.

Coons's thinking went as follows: Let the curves be given in a rectangular network such as the following:

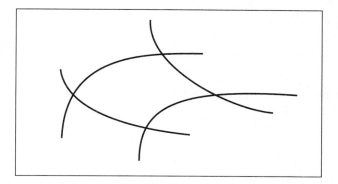

Coons defined two "lofted" surfaces $s_1(u,v)$ and $s_2(u,v)$. These are ruled surfaces made from the pair of parallel curves; thus, $s_1(u,v)$ is a bundle of linearly interpolated "rulings" from one curve to the other, such as the following:

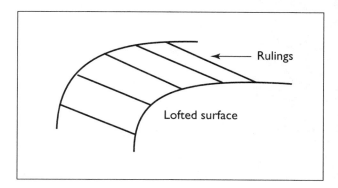

The surface $s_2(u,v)$ is ruled in the other direction, that is, with the other two curves.

The two surfaces s_1 and s_2 each interpolate to two pairs of curves. The goal, however, is to devise a patch that interpolates to all four curves. Coons's insight was to find a third surface s_3 such that the surface $s = s_1 + s_2 - s_3$ would result in the desired property. Surface s_3 is just the bilinear interpolant (Bézier) patch of the four corner points.

The surface between the boundary curves is a bilinearly blended surface called a Coons patch. Because it interpolates curves, not just points, it is an example of what is known as transfinite interpolation.

The Coons patch can "fill in" any rectangular network of parametric curves. Higher-order analogs of the bilinearly blended Coons patch achieve different continuity orders between patches.

Finally, if the parametric curves given are Bézier curves, then the Coons patch of those curves will reduce to the Bézier patch. Therefore, the Coons patch is a generalization of the Bézier patch. See [Farin93] for more details on the Coons patch.

The "Gregory patch" [Hosaka84] [Chiyokura83] may be thought of as a blend of two Bézier patches using rational blending terms. Consider two sets of bicubic Bézier control points. The points around the boundary are identical in both sets; only the four interior control points differ. To illustrate:

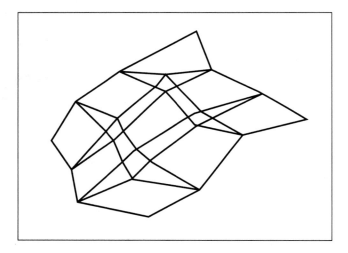

The figure shows the control mesh of one patch that is blended with the mesh of another.

The actual Gregory patch is a rational blend of the two patches. The boundaries are clearly the same. For the bicubic case, the patch becomes rational and may be described as a degree 4 polynomial divided by a degree 7 polynomial.

The advantage of this patch is that it is easy to match derivatives and twist vectors (mixed partials) across the boundary with adjacent patches. This includes patches that may meet in nonrectangular networks, for example, where three patches meet at a vertex. Gregory patches are especially useful for combining irregular configurations of patches [Hosaka84].

Nonrectangular Patches

So far, every surface considered has had a rectangular arrangement: four corner points, four boundary curves, and two orthogonal parameters. Unfortunately not all objects accommodate a rectangular topology; try to cover a sphere with rectangles. This is difficult to do without producing degenerate rectangular patches at the poles, but these are no longer rectangular and they cause many computational problems, such as no defined derivatives.

Consider what happens at the poles in the following figure:

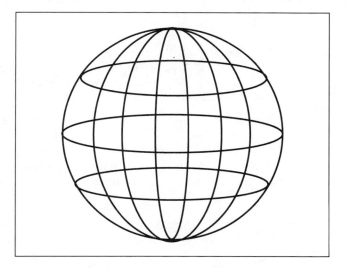

The following figure exhibits regions that are triangular, rectangular, and hexagonal. It also possesses five-sided regions.

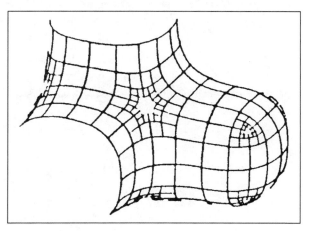

To solve these topological problems, a variety of different patch types have been suggested.

Triangular Patches

It became clear early in the development of surface design that a good triangular patch would solve all topological problems. Any region, including rectangular, could be configured from triangular patches. [Sabin76] was the first detailed treatment of triangular patches, while [Farin86] and [Gregory80] provide clear explanations. Triangular patches have, however, been particularly difficult to make smooth across boundaries while maintaining low degree.

The Clough-Tocher [Barnhill74] and Sabin-Powell [Powell77] patches split the triangular patches into smaller triangular subpatches to generate degrees of freedom for continuity purposes. Clough-Tocher does a three-way split with cubic subpatches, and Sabin-Powell does a nine-way split with quadratic pieces.

Many researchers have investigated multisided patches made from rectangular patches [Sabin86], [Varady87]. The modeler DESIGNBASE [Chiyokura86] uses Gregory patches in different arrangements to create multisided patches, including triangular. The Gregory patches endow the system with good boundary smoothness. The following figure shows three- and five-sided Gregory patch arrangements:

There are numerous other composition schemes such as [Varady91], [Varady95], and [Zhao94].

Direct definition of triangular patches has followed from attempts to extend rectangular methods. There is a triangular Coons patch approach, a triangular Bézier approach, and a triangular B-spline approach [Nielson79], [Nielson87], [Bloor91], [Varady91], and [Farin86].

While mathematically important, none of the triangular surfaces exist in a successful modeling system. One problem seems to be a concentration of high curvature along the boundaries, in spite of mathematically defined smoothness.

Direct definition of a general multisided patch includes methods by [Loop90], [Plowman95], [Charrot84], [Varady87], and [Boehm83]. These methods tend to be computationally expensive and require special handling routines.

One method to handle multisided regions that occur is recursive subdivision [Doo78], [Filip86], [Nasri91], and [Catmull78]. In this method, a polyhedral object is successively chamfered along its edges, such as in the following example.

First, the original object:

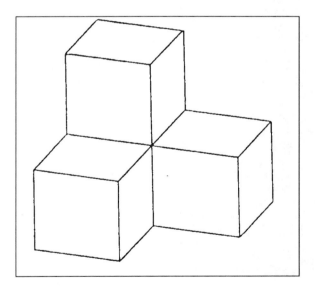

Now, after the first stage of chamfering:

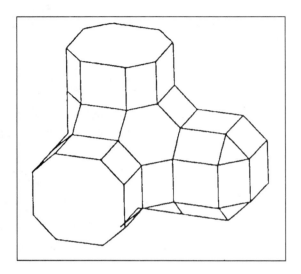

After the second stage of chamfering:

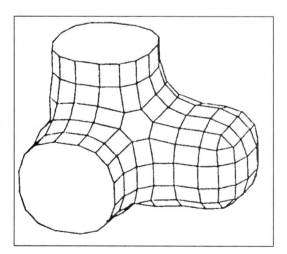

The following figure shows a real example: an automobile component, before and after chamfering.

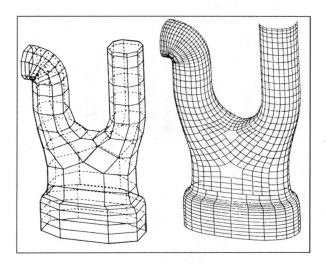

Anomalous regions, such as the triangles above, get squeezed out by the chamfering process as smaller and smaller rectangular regions form around them. Adjoining rectangular regions eventually converge to a B-spline surface patch that can be replaced whenever it occurs. Finally, all but the vanishing anomalous regions are converted to B-spline patches.

This is illustrated in the following figure:

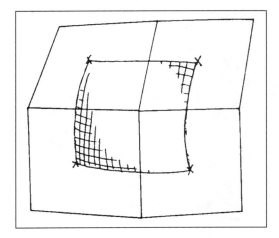

The method provides an intuitive interface for designing sculptured objects, but the large numbers of patches in some regions, together with the small anomalous regions, create numerical and topological problems for the method.

Other Surface Definitions

Although it is not exactly another surface type, trimmed surfaces are a popular method for extending regular Bézier and B-spline surfaces. To trim a surface, a region of the parameter space is cut away or trimmed, usually by defining a curve. One side of the curve is considered part of the surface, while the other side is not. The trimmed region is then mapped to the surface. The result is a surface that looks like it has some regions removed.

So far, all curves and surfaces have been defined with parametric forms. There is, however, a large body of surface types that are defined implicitly.

An implicit surface is defined as the zero set of a function that maps from 3-space to the real numbers; a curve may be defined by a function from 2-space to the real numbers. For instance, the unit circle is given by the zero set of

$$f(\mathbf{x}) = x^2 + y^2 + z^2 - 1,$$

where $\mathbf{x} = (x,y,z)$. The zero set is the set of $\mathbf{x}$ such that $f(\mathbf{x}) = 0$.

Many common engineering surfaces are defined simply and effectively by implicit functions such as the plane, sphere, cylinder, cone, and torus.

A Bézier formulation for implicit surfaces was given by [Sederberg85]. This has since led to many schemes with a form of control point interface that patch together complex surfaces. [Dahman89] and [Bajaj95] are examples.

Implicit surfaces have advantages related to their implicit form of definition. It is easy, for example, to determine an inside and an outside of an implicit surface by simply testing for $f(\mathbf{x}) < 0$ or $f(\mathbf{x}) > 0$. If a point $\mathbf{x}$ is on the surface, then $f(\mathbf{x}) = 0$. In order to make the same determination for a parametric surface, the parameters of the surface must be found that yield the desired point on the surface, or a point close to the desired point if it is off the surface. This can be a difficult "inversion" problem.

Another advantage of implicit surfaces is that the gradient of the function yields a vector that is normal to the surface, useful for rendering.

Finally, implicit surfaces naturally define a distance; that is, $f(\mathbf{x})$ may be thought of as measuring the distance from $\mathbf{x}$ to the zero surface. This feature is very useful in designing a class of blending or filleting surfaces that form transition surfaces between surfaces that would otherwise join along a corner or sharp edge [Rockwood89].

Implicit and Parametric Surfaces

Because each form of surface has its own set of advantages, it is appropriate to end this section by considering the question, what surfaces have both an implicit and parametric form so that advantage can be taken of both?

In the case of curves, conic splines have been defined with both forms [Pavlidis83]. For surfaces, clearly the plane, circle, cylinder, torus, and a few other simple forms have this property. Cyclides are surfaces that are found on generalized toruses that have a variable minor radius [Pratt90] and [Chandru89]. They can be fitted smoothly together under certain constraints and have useful representations in both forms.

[Sederberg83] used classical mathematics [Salmon1885] to show how any polynomial surface could be converted from parametric to implicit form. [Goldman85] expanded upon this subject. Unfortunately, the results also show that unwieldy polynomials may result. A bicubic patch in parametric form may have 324 terms in implicit form. More recent work, however, has shown a useful subset of surfaces with far fewer terms [Sederberg95].

WHAT HAS BEEN ACCOMPLISHED IN THIS TOPIC

A wide variety of curves and surfaces exist apart from the standard Bézier and B-spline types, and new ideas are appearing constantly. This topic has given a view of the less common curves and surfaces, and suggests many places for the interested reader to study further.

Bibliography

[Bajaj95] C. Bajaj and G. Xu. Modeling with cubic A patches. *ACM Trans. on Graphics*, 1995.

[Barnhill74] R. Barnhill. Smooth interpolation over triangles. In R. Barnhill and R. Riesenfeld, editors, *Computer Aided Geometric Design*, pages 45–70, Academic Press, Boston, 1974. This volume contains the proceedings of the first conference on CAGD.

[Barnhill82] R. Barnhill. Coons patches. *Computers in Industry* 3: 37–43, 1982.

[Barsky81] B. Barsky. *The Beta-spline: A Local Representation Based on Shape Parameters and Fundamental Geometric Measures.* Ph.D. thesis, Dept. of Computer Science, University of Utah, 1981.

[Bartels87] R. Bartels, J. Beatty, and B. Barsky. *An Introduction of Splines for Use in Computer Graphics and Geometric Modeling.* Morgan Kaufmann, San Francisco, 1987.

[Blinn78] J. Blinn. Simulation of wrinkled surfaces. *Computer Graphics* 12(3): 286–292, 1978.

[Bloor91] M. Bloor and M. Wilson. Generating blending surfaces with partial differential equations, *Computer Aided Design*, 25: 251–256, 1991.

[Boehm83] W. Boehm and G. Farin. Concerning subdivision of Bézier triangles. *Computer Aided Design* 15(5): 260–261, 1983. Letter to the editor.

[Boehm84] W. Boehm, G. Farin, and J. Kahmann. A survey of curve and surface methods in CAGD. *Computer Aided Geometric Design* 1(1): 1–60, 1984.

[Catmull74] E. Catmull. *A Subdivision Algorithm for the Computer Display of Curved Surfaces.* Ph.D. thesis, Dept. of Computer Science, University of Utah, 1974.

[Catmull78] E. Catmull and J. Clark. Recursively generated B-spline surfaces on arbitrary topological meshes. *Computer Aided Design* 10(6): 350–355, 1978.

[Catmull & Rom74] E. Catmull and R. Rom. A class of local interpolating splines. In R. Barnhill and R. Riesenfeld, editors, *Computer Aided Geometric Design*, pages 317–326, Academic Press, Boston, 1974.

[Charrot84] P. Charrot and J. Gregory. A pentagonal surface patch for computer aided geometric design. *Computer Aided Geometric Design* 1(1): 87–94, 1984.

[Chandru89] V. Chandru, D. Dutta, and C. M. Hoffmann. On the geometry of dupin cyclides. *The Visual Computer* 5(5): 277–290, 1989.

[Chiyokura83] H. Chiyokura and F. Kimura. Design of solids with free-form surfaces. *Computer Graphics* 17(3): 289–298, 1983.

[Chiyokura86] H. Chiyokura. *Solid Modeling with Designbase, Theory and Implementation.* Addison Wesley, New York, 1986.

[Coons64] S. Coons. Surfaces for computer aided design. Technical report, MIT, 1964. Available as AD 663 504 from the National Technical Information Service, Springfield, VA 22161. This is the first of Coons's papers on his patch.

[Dahman89] W. Dahman. Smooth piecewise quadric shapes. In *Mathematical Methods in CAGD.* T. Lyche, L. Schumaker, editors, Academic Press, Boston, 1989.

[deBoor78] C. de Boor. *A Practical Guide to Splines.* Springer, New York, 1978. This is the classical reference to splines written for the numerical analyst.

[Doo78] D. Doo and M. Sabin. Behavior of recursive division surfaces near extra-ordinary points. *Computer Aided Design* 10(6): 356–360, 1978.

[Farin86] G. Farin. Triangular Bernstein-Bézier patches. *Computer Aided Geometric Design* 3(2): 83–128, 1986.

[Farin93] G. Farin. *Curves and Surfaces for Computer Aided Geometric Design.* Third edition. Academic Press, Boston, 1993. This is the popular work specifically on parametric curves and surfaces.

[Faux79] I. Faux and M. Pratt. *Computational Geometry for Design and Manufacture.* Ellis Horwood, U.K., 1979. This is the first text on the subject, still an interesting read.

[Filip86] D. Filip. Adaptive subdivision algorithms for a set of Bézier triangles. *Computer Aided Design* 18(2): 74–78, 1986.

[Foley92] J. Foley and A. Van Dam. *Fundamentals of Interactive Computer Graphics.* Addison-Wesley, New York, 1992. A popular textbook on computer graphics, this text has a few introductory chapters on CAGD.

[Forrest72] A. Forrest. On Coons's and other methods for the representation of curved surfaces. *Computer Graphics and Image Processing* 1(4): 341–359, 1972.

[Goldman85] R. Goldman. The method of resolvents: a technique for the implic-itization, inversion, and intersection of non-planar, parametric, rational cubic curves. *Computer Aided Geometric Design* 2(4): 237–255, 1985.

[Goldman88] R. Goldman. Urn models, approximations and splines. *Journal of Approximation Theory* 54: 1–66, 1988.

[Goshtasby93] A. Goshtasby. Design and recovery of 2D and 3D shapes using rational Gaussian curves and surfaces. *International Journal of Computer Vision* 10(3): 233–256, 1993.

[Gregory80] J. Gregory and P. Charrot. A C_1 triangular interpolation patch for com-puter-aided geometric design. *Computer Graphics and Image Processing* 13(1): 80–87, 1980.

[Hoffmann89] C. Hoffmann. *Geometric & Solid Modeling*. Morgan Kaufmann, San Francisco, 1989.

[Hosaka84] M. Hosaka and F. Kimura. Non-four-sided patch expressions with control points. *Computer Aided Geometric Design* 1(1): 75–86, 1984.

[Hoschek89] J. Hoschek and K. Lasser. *Grundlagen der Geometrischen Datenverarbeiturng*. B.G. Teubner, Stuttgart, 1989. English translation: *Fundamentals of Computer Aided Geometric Design*, Jones and Bartlett, Boston. This is a very broad and comprehensive text.

[Loop90] C. Loop and T. DeRose. Generalized B-spline surfaces of arbitrary topology. *Computer Graphics* 24(4): 347–356, 1990.

[Nasri91] A. Nasri. Boundary-corner control in recursive-subdivision surfaces. *Computer Aided Design* 23(6): 405–410, 1991.

[Nielson79] G. Nielson. The side-vertex method for interpolation in triangles. *Journal of Approximation Theory* 25: 318–336, 1979.

[Nielson86] G. Nielson. A rectangular nu-spline for interactive surface design. *IEEE Computer Graphics and Applications* 6(2): 35–41, 1986.

[Nielson87] G. Nielson. A transfinite, visually continuous, triangular interpolant. In G. Farin, editor, *Geometric Modeling: Algorithms and New Trends*, pages 235–246, SIAM, Philadelphia, 1987.

[Pavlidis83] T. Pavlidis. Curve fitting with conic splines. *ACM Transactions on Graphics* 2(1): 1–31, 1983.

[Plowman95] D. Plowman and P. Charrot. A practical implementation of vertex blend surfaces using an n-sided patch. In G. Mullineux, editor, *The Mathematics of Surfaces*, VI, Oxford University Press, Oxford, 1995.

[Powell77] M. Powell and M. Sabin. Piecewise quadratic approximations on triangles. *ACM Transactions on Mathematical Software* 3: 316–325, 1977.

[Pratt90] M. Pratt. Cyclides in computer aided geometric design. *Computer Aided Geometric Design* 7(1–4): 221–242, 1990.

[Rockwood89] A. Rockwood. The displacement method for implicit blending surfaces in solid models. *ACM Transactions on Graphics* 8(4): 279–297, 1989.

[Sabin76] M. Sabin. *The Use of Piecewise Forms for the Numerical Representation of Shape.* Ph.D. thesis, Hungarian Academy of Sciences, Budapest, Hungary, 1976.

[Sabin86] M. Sabin. Some negative results in n-sided patches. *Computer Aided Design* 18(1): 38–44, 1986.

[Salmon1885] G. Salmon. *Modern Higher Algebra.* Fifth edition. Chelsea, New York, pp. 83–86, 1885. An excellent Victorian text on geometry. Be careful how you name books; notice the date!

[Sederberg83] T. Sederberg. *Implicit and Parametric Curves and Surfaces for Computer Aided Geometric Design.* Ph.D. thesis, Purdue University, 1983.

[Sederberg85] T. Sederberg. Piecewise algebraic surface patches. *Computer Aided Geometric Design 2,* 1985.

[Sederberg95] T. Sederberg. Implicitization using moving curves and surfaces. *Proc. of ACM SIGGRAPH '95,* August 1995.

[Varady87] T. Varady. Survey and new results in n-sided patch generation. in R. Martin, editor, *The Mathematics of Surfaces II,* pages 203–236, Oxford University Press, Oxford, 1987.

[Varady91] T. Varady. Overlap patches: a new scheme for interpolating curve networks with n-sided regions. *Computer Aided Geometric Design* 8: 7–27, 1991.

[Varady95] T. Varady and A. Rockwood. Vertex blending based on the setback split. *Mathematical Methods in CAGD III,* M. Daehlen et al., editors, Vanderbilt University Press, 1995.

[Zhao94] Y. Zhao and A. Rockwood. A convolution approach to N-sided patches and vertex blending. In N. Sapidis, editor, *Designing Fair Curves and Surfaces,* SIAM, Philadelphia, 1994.

Solutions
to Exercises

2.1   For example, a car makes a smooth turn on a road.

2.2   For example, a car slows to a stop sign, turns its wheels, and then speeds up again in a different direction.

2.3   For example, a baton is passed from one runner to a faster runner, who stays in the same lane of the track.

2.4 $\mathbf{l}(0) = \mathbf{b}_0$.

2.5 $\mathbf{l}(1) = \mathbf{b}_1$.

2.6 $\mathbf{l}(0.5) = \dfrac{\mathbf{b}_0 + \mathbf{b}_1}{2}$.

3.1   *Hint:* Start with the simple quadratic form, and extend the solution to a general form.

4.1   One example is slalom skiing, where the prime objective is to "interpolate" the flags down the slope. Another example is croquet, where the ball must go through the hoops, regardless of any other moves it makes.

4.2   They share the same direction, but the Hermite tangent vector is n times the length of the first leg of the Bézier polygon, where n is the degree of the curve.

4.3   There are many ways, given that the end vector of a given segment must match the start vector of the next segment.

One way is to take the central difference, that is

$$\mathbf{m}_i = \alpha(\mathbf{p}_{i+1} - \mathbf{p}_{i-1}),$$

where α is an appropriate scalar constant.

Special care must be taken with the first and last vectors of the set of segments.

4.4   The derivative of the Bézier curve at the endpoints is given by

$$\mathbf{p}'(0) = 3\Delta\mathbf{b}_0, \ \mathbf{p}'(1) = 3\Delta\mathbf{b}_2.$$

The intermediate points can easily be determined:

$$\mathbf{b}_1 = \mathbf{p}_0 + \frac{1}{3}\mathbf{m}_0, \mathbf{b}_2 = \mathbf{p}_1 + \frac{1}{3}\mathbf{m}_1.$$

This gives the Bézier form of the curve:

$$\mathbf{p}(t) = \mathbf{p}_0 B_0^3(t) + \left(\mathbf{p}_0 + \frac{1}{3}\mathbf{m}_0\right)B_1^3(t) + \left(\mathbf{p}_1 - \frac{1}{3}\mathbf{m}_1\right)B_2^3(t) + \mathbf{p}_1 B_3^3(t).$$

To get the Hermite form, substitute

$$\mathbf{p}(t) = \mathbf{p}_0 H_0^3 (t) + \mathbf{m}_0 H_1^3 (t) + \mathbf{m}_1 H_2^3 (t) + \mathbf{p}_1 H_3^3 (t).$$

This gives the Hermite basis functions.

4.5   The Hermite form possesses

■ endpoint interpolation

■ Affine invariance

This property arises trivially, since there are only two points in the Hermite equation, **p**0 and **p**1. **m**0 and **m**1 are vectors determined by the points and are not transformed directly.

5.1   Here is a typical answer:

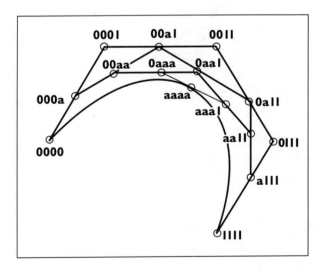

5.2a   The blossom of

$$5u^3 + u^2$$

is given by

$$5u_1u_2u_3 = \frac{u_1u_2 + u_2u_3 + u_1u_3}{3}.$$

5.2b   The blossom of

$$\mathbf{b}u^2 + 2$$

is given by:

$$\mathbf{b}u_1u_2 + 2.$$

5.3   See Topic 6, "The B-Spline Curve."

6.1   The following figure gives the answer:

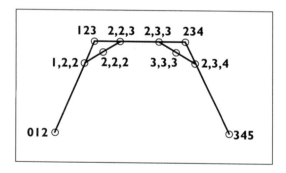

6.2   The following figure gives the answer. The points 000 and 111 define a portion of the curve that is not part of the B-spline.

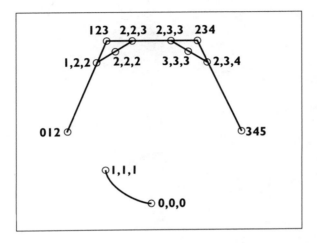

Index

About the Authors

Alyn P. Rockwood completed B.S. and M.S. degrees in mathematics at Brigham Young University and a Ph.D. at the Department of Applied Mathematics and Theoretical Physics of Cambridge University, Cambridge, England. He worked in industrial research for 13 years, including supervisory and research positions at Evans and Sutherland Computer Corporation and Silicon Graphics, Inc. He was involved in flight simulation, CAD/CAM, and surface-rendering projects at these companies.

Currently, Alyn is on the computer science faculty at Arizona State University. His interests include computer graphics, scientific visualization, computer-aided geometric design, and image processing. He has several patents and many publications in these fields.

Peter Chambers received his B.Sc. from the University of Exeter, England, and his M.S. from Arizona State University. Peter has worked in the areas of digital design and computer architecture for 15 years and is presently an engineering fellow in the Advanced Multimedia Development Group at VLSI Technology Inc., Tempe, Arizona. His areas of expertise at VLSI include circuit design, bus architectures, and peripheral interfaces for personal computers.

Peter has architected and designed numerous products, including the Input/Output System for minicomputers, and many large integrated circuits. Peter's other interests include high-level hardware description languages, techniques for robust design, and interface performance analysis.

Peter's involvement with Arizona State University includes research on texturing methods in computer graphics and interactive learning tools for CAGD and computer graphics.

Related Titles from Morgan Kaufmann

Principles of Digital Image Synthesis

Andrew S. Glassner, Microsoft Research

A comprehensive presentation of the three core fields of study that constitute digital image synthesis: the human visual system, digital signal processing, and the interaction of matter and light. Assuming no more than a basic background in calculus, Glassner demonstrates how these disciplines are elegantly orchestrated into modern rendering techniques such as radiosity and ray tracing.

1995; 1600 pages; two-volume set; cloth; 1-55860-276-3

Geometric & Solid Modeling: An Introduction

Christoph M. Hoffmann, Purdue University

This book deals with the concepts and tools needed to design and implement solid modeling systems and their infrastructure and substrata, making this information remarkably accessible—to the novice as well as to the experienced designer. The essential algorithms and the underlying theory needed to design these systems are given primary emphasis.

1989; 335 pages; cloth; ISBN 1-55860-067-1

Making Them Move: Mechanics, Control and Animation of Articulated Figures

Edited by Norman I. Badler, Brian A. Barsky, and David Zeltzer

Making Them Move presents the work of leading researchers on movement from computer graphics, psychology, robotics and mechanical engineering. It explores biological and robotic motor control, as well as state-of-the-art computer graphics techniques for simulating human and animal figures in a natural and physically realistic manner. The accompanying one-hour videotape includes selected animation sequences demonstrating these techniques.

1990; Book/Video Package: ISBN 1-55860-155-4

Book Only: 348 pages; cloth; ISBN 1-55860-106-6

Videotape Only: 1 hour, VHS or PAL; ISBN 1-55860-154-6